Everyday Life
in Ottoman Turkey

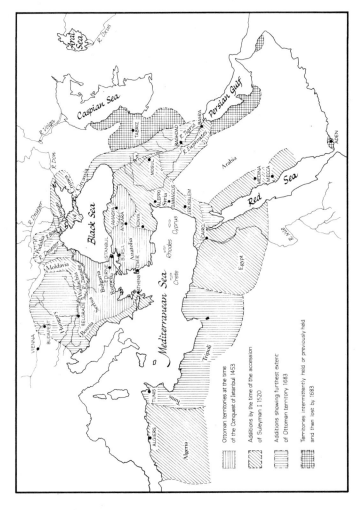

Map of the Ottoman Empire

Ottoman territories at the time
of the Conquest of Istanbul 1453

Additions by the time of the accession
of Suleyman I 1520

Additions showing furthest extent
of Ottoman territory 1683

Territories intermittently held or previously held
and then lost by 1683

Everyday Life in

OTTOMAN
TURKEY

Raphaela Lewis

B. T. BATSFORD LTD London
G. P. PUTNAM'S SONS New York

To my family

First published 1971
© Raphaela Lewis, 1971
7134 1687 4
Printed and bound in Great Britain by
Jarrold and Sons Ltd, Norwich and London
for the publishers
B. T. BATSFORD LTD
4 Fitzhardinge Street, London W1H OAH
G. P. PUTNAM'S SONS
200 Madison Avenue, New York, NY 10016

56, H26

CONTENTS

THE ILLUSTRATIONS

ACKNOWLEDGMENT

In Turkish fashion, help with this book came almost entirely from family and friends, so it is with affection as well as gratitude that I thank Shevket Rado, publisher of *Hayat Mecmuasi*, Nejat Sönmez, Niyazi Babur and Ziya Tugal of the Directorate-General of Press and Information of the Prime Minister's Office, Ankara, and Godfrey Goodwin, for the generosity that made available so many of the illustrations, as well as Sheila Lewis for her meticulous help in the preparation of the typescript and the reading of the proofs. I am similarly indebted to Dr. Richard C. Repp for his advice on the historical material, and particularly those aspects on which information is not yet readily available. Of the goodness and patience of my husband, Geoffrey Lewis, who made accessible both his encyclopaedic knowledge of sources and his own scholarship and insights, who directed my researches and evaluated my conclusions, I can hardly write.

The author and publisher also wish to thank the following for permission to reproduce the illustrations appearing in this book:
The Ashmolean Museum, Oxford, for fig. 3.
The Bodleian Library, Oxford, for fig. 12.
The Turkish Tourism and Information Office, London, for fig. 58.
The Directorate-General of Press and Information, Ankara, for figs. 2, 5, 13, 33, 35, 38, 39, 47, 50–52, 60, 61, 65, 70.
Other illustrations include engravings by Thomas Allom *(Constantinople and the Scenery of the Seven Churches of Asia Minor*, London and Paris, 1838), Edward William Lane *(An Account of the Manners and Customs of the Modern Egyptians*, London 1836 and editions), Antoine Ignace Melling *(Voyage pittoresque de Constantinople et des rives du Bosphore*, Paris, 1819), and W. H. Bartlett (in Miss Pardoe's *The Beauties of the Bosphorus*, London 1839), a few old and unidentifiable prints and postcards, and line drawings and photographs by the author.

OTTOMAN SULTANS

Osman I	1281–1324	Murad IV	1623–1640
Orhan	1324–1362	Ibrahim	1640–1648
Murad I	1362–1389	Mehmed IV	1648–1687
Bayezid I	1389–1402	Suleyman II	1687–1691
(Interregnum)		Ahmed II	1691–1695
		Mustafa II	1695–1703
Mehmed I	1413–1421	Ahmed III	1703–1730
Murad II	1421–1444;	Mahmud I	1730–1754
	1446–1451	Osman III	1754–1757
Mehmed II	1444–1446;	Mustafa III	1757–1774
	1451–1481	Abdulhamid I	1774–1789
Bayezid II	1481–1512	Selim III	1789–1807
Selim I	1512–1520	Mustafa IV	1807–1808
Suleyman I	1520–1566	Mahmud II	1808–1839
Selim II	1566–1574	Abdulmejid	1839–1861
Murad III	1574–1595	Abdulaziz	1861–1876
Mehmed III	1595–1603	Murad V	1876
Ahmed I	1603–1617	Abdulhamid II	1876–1909
Mustafa I	1617–1618;	Mehmed V	1909–1918
	1622–1623	Mehmed VI	1918–1922
Osman II	1618–1622	Abdulmejid II	1922–1924

I

Ottoman Turkey, its History and People

In the sixth century, from their homeland somewhere west of the Great Wall of China, the Turks rode out to begin the conquests that were to give their descendants mastery of one of the greatest empires the world has ever seen. Although they were originally animists, worshippers of earth, sky and water, they fell at various times under the influences of Buddhism, Manichaeism, Judaism and Christianity as they made their way into Central Asia and Eastern Europe. The advances of the Mongols drove them into the Arab empire and here they found the religion of Islam, the faith which was to become their inspiration. The Muslim religion represented a way of life which was ideally suited to these fighting men, since it comprised a code of behaviour which called for implicit obedience and few decisions, and offered great rewards both in this life and hereafter for soldiers who fought and died in the holy war. Since, too, profession of the Muslim faith automatically conferred membership of a vast and successful community it had a cohesive effect on otherwise disparate bodies of conquerors and conquered, and resulted in an almost invincible solidarity. With the adoption of Islam these splendid Turkish fighters now had a religious as well as territorial incentive for going into battle, and Persia, Mesopotamia, Syria and Anatolia fell before them.

This vigorous expansion of Turkish power coincided with the decline of eastern Christendom. The empire of 'New Rome, which is Constantinople' had been weakened economically as her possessions were lost to the Venetians and Genoese as well as to the encroaching Turks, and militarily as her army shrank and her defences became enfeebled. The Fourth Crusade which captured and looted Constantinople, the capital of the Byzantine Empire, confirmed the bitterness which had long existed between the Latin Church, who owed allegiance to the Pope, and the Greek Orthodox Church whose Patriarch was subordinate to their Emperor. The combination of factors which disorganised and divided Christendom left no united resistance strong enough to withstand a steady stream of predatory and determined invaders from the Muslim east, and the Turks advanced inexorably.

Of the various dynasties who ruled them as they expanded and flourished during this time the most powerful was that of the Seljuks, a nomad horde which had swarmed westward, crushing all rivals, driving back the Crusaders and reuniting Muslim Asia. From 1037 to 1300 they ruled brilliantly an empire which at its greatest reached from Afghanistan to the Mediterranean. Eventually, however, they too fell victim to the might of the Mongols and to inner disintegration, and their power declined until only the Seljuks of Rum, of Asia Minor, remained. But while the central government was losing control, small, strong groups of tribesmen were establishing themselves in Anatolia. There had always been organisations of Ghazis, or Fighters for the Faith, who, becoming restless when the lands which they had conquered became settled, constantly broke away and advanced to extend the boundaries of Islam. By the thirteenth century a number of independent bands of Ghazis had ensconced themselves in principalities which owed almost no allegiance to the Seljuks or their Mongol overlords who held the interior. Such a band was that of Ertughrul, father of Othman, who founded the Ottoman dynasty. And here history and legend become confused, to produce the following story.

Ertughrul, great warrior of a noble line, born to rule, was leading his tribe of 400 horsemen across the Anatolian plateau when he came upon a battle in which the sides were very unevenly matched. He gallantly led his men to the aid of the smaller army, and together they won the day. The leader of the side he had helped was, it transpired, none other than Alauddin Kaikobad, the Sultan of the Seljuks of Rum, who in gratitude gave Ertughrul a grant of land along the Byzantine frontier in the extreme north-west of his territory. Ertughrul was to be Warden of the Marches, to hold the territory for the Sultan and extend it if he could.

This account, while dramatised in many details, nevertheless demonstrates the way in which small, powerful, nomadic groups were able to establish themselves in Asia Minor, both because of their own strength and because the failing Seljuk empire was glad of their support against the Mongol threat from the east and Christianity in the west.

But nothing could now save the last of the Seljuks. The invasion of Asia Minor by the Mongol conqueror Genghis Khan reduced their sultan to a mere tributary ruler, and the fresh bands of Turkish immigrants, swept forward by the Mongol advances, increased the general disorder, so that by the end of the thirteenth century the country was in a state almost of anarchy, with control in the hands of a number of virtually independent chieftains. One of these was Osman, whose name was pronounced Othman in Arabic; from this 'Ottoman', which is common western usage, appears to be derived. He succeeded his father Ertughrul in 1281, and when he declared his independence of Seljuk authority, reputedly in 1299, this was the simple statement of a fact which the Seljuks were powerless to deny. Osman then began his career of conquest, and although his was originally one of the weakest of the numerous states that were to divide up the kingdom of Rum among themselves, within a hundred years the house of Osman had swept away most of their rivals and founded the Empire that was to bear their famous name for 600 years.

Osman's son Orkhan, who succeeded him, adopted the title of Sultan and coined Turkish money to replace the Byzantine and Seljuk currency. It was he who reorganised the army, which had up to then consisted of volunteer horsemen who returned to their villages after campaigns. He linked a cavalry militia to land tenure so that fief-holders were obliged to serve in war, and at a moment's notice, with a following including horses and equipment, proportionate to the size of their land holding. Unlike those in Western Europe these fiefs were not hereditary, and the land was held directly from the ruler, to whom alone allegiance was owed.

The reason for the early success and enduring power of the Ottomans is not far to seek. The frontier of Byzantium, where Ertughrul's tribe had settled, was the most vulnerable spot in Christendom, and the steady stream of ghazis pouring in from all parts of Anatolia to fight the enemies of Islam were naturally attracted to the expanding Osmanli state, from which they could attack, loot and possibly convert the infidel Balkan kingdoms to which it was the gateway. The Osmanlis gave them the work to do that they liked best, and reaped the advantages. The defences of Byzantium itself had become enfeebled, and its army small—between 10,000 and 12,000 men—and unreliable, and in the late thirteenth and early fourteenth centuries the Byzantine provinces had disintegrated socially and economically. The Balkan peninsula, which had been racked by rival pretenders, warring nobles and deep-rooted social and religious strife, was ripe for conquest. Much of the land was held by monasteries and absentee landlords, and as the Turkish conquerors 'liberated' it and turned it over to the destitute peasants they were hailed as deliverers. By wiping out the big land-owners the Turks put an end to the old feudalism in the Balkans and opened new horizons to the small farmers, who settled gratefully under Turkish rule and rewarded their benefactors with their loyalty. In fact many Bogomils who had been persecuted by both Catholics and Greek Orthodox turned to the Turks as their saviours, and adopted Islam.

As the Ottomans realised how rich and disunited Europe was, they advanced further, eventually establishing firm domination over Thrace and the Balkans. As these conquests were consolidated, the ulema, the established heads of law and religion, moved in to organise the administration of the new territories, thereby establishing order and stability, which brought in turn conformity, strength and permanence. Indeed, towards the end of the fourteenth century the Ottoman Empire held more territory in Europe than in Asia. In 1390, however, Sultan Bayezid began his conquests in Asia Minor. His Muslim troops were unwilling to fight their co-religionists, whom, anyway, they could not loot with a clear conscience, so Bayezid reinforced his army with vassal Serbs and Greeks. Though the Sultan advanced rapidly in Asia Minor during the last decade of the fourteenth century, his conquests there were swept away in 1402 following his crushing defeat near Ankara at the hands of the great Mongol conqueror Timur. It was to be nearly three-quarters of a century before the Ottomans were fully to recover the lands so rapidly won and even more rapidly lost.

The disaster at Ankara did not materially affect the Ottoman possessions in Europe, however, where they continued their advance during the first half of the fifteenth century; but the great prize, Constantinople, was still to be won. Impoverished by the capture of its rich provinces and its taxation revenues, cut off by the loss of Anatolia from the supply of soldiers for its armies, the East Roman Empire was now a pitiful remnant, surrounded by the powerful and successful Turks. Its greatest weakness perhaps lay in the jealous dissension between the Latins and the Greeks. Although in 1439 its Emperor John VIII accepted the supremacy of the Pope and the union of the Greek and Latin Churches, hoping for help against the Turks, the Byzantine clergy and the devout Orthodox citizens of Constantinople fiercely rejected any compromise with the hated Latins as a betrayal of orthodoxy. Even on the eve of the Turkish conquest it was the Pope who was the real enemy, and indeed such help as the Christian princes sent to the beleaguered city was totally inadequate. When, in 1452, Mehmed II completed the building of the fortress of Rumeli Hisar, closing the Bosphorus to Constantinople, the people of the city prepared for their last stand in a spirit of despair. Mehmed II had the first real artillery park in history: an array of bombards and cannon, as well as an enormous army including levies from Europe and Asia, and 100,000 irregulars and camp followers, while the population of Constantinople at this time was some 60–70,000, of whom 5,000 prepared to fight. In answer to the Emperor Constantine's desperate plea the Pope sent Cardinal Isidore and 200 soldiers. At the Cardinal's first act, which was the promulgation of a Dictum of Union in the great church of St Sophia, including the name of the Pope, the populace rejected him with the furious cry of: 'Better the turban of the Turk than the Pope's tiara.' The Genoese sent 3,000 troops, and Constantine courageously prepared to do battle, but his army was still totally inadequate to man the walls and repair the breaches.

The city was defended by a three-tier wall interspersed with moats and set with towers and broad enclosures for the movement of troops.

1. *Three tiered wall of Theodosius (5th Century)*
2. *Chain across entrance to Golden Horn*
3. *Ships carried overland*
4. *First Turkish breach in the walls*

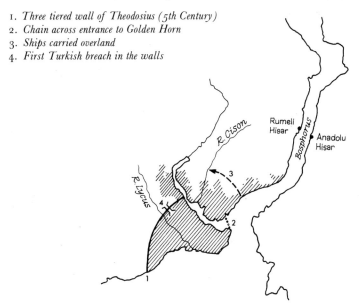

1   The fortifications of Constantinople at the time of the Conquest

These walls had defied twenty sieges but were now to meet their match. The entrance to the Golden Horn was protected by a great chain which stretched from shore to shore. Mehmed's master-stroke was to construct a greased wooden runway which ran from the Bosphorus to a stream which flowed into the Golden Horn. Over this seventy or eighty ships were dragged by oxen, slipped into the stream and floated down the Golden Horn into the harbour, within the chain. The population woke on Easter Monday, 1453, to the terrifying spectacle of a hostile navy bobbing about inside their city.

Fierce fighting raged for days, but on 29th May Mehmed ordered a simultaneous attack on the land and sea walls. The land walls were finally breached, and the Emperor Constantine died fighting there. All the Greek and Italian soldiers who had been trapped between the walls were massacred, and the Turks rushed into the city and indulged in three days of merciless pillage and plunder—although even this was probably not so destructive as the sack of the city by the Crusaders had been. Then Mehmed firmly restored order and declared, to the surprise of those who had expected him to raze the city to the ground, that he would make Constantinople the capital of his empire.

It must not be thought that the Turks at the time of the capture of Constantinople were wild barbarians: their beautiful capital at Bursa was testimony to their skill in the arts and architecture. Also, of course, the Ottomans and the Byzantines had been near neighbours for over a century and there had been many cultural and indeed matrimonial exchanges, and even occasional reciprocal military help and alliances.

One of Mehmed's first acts on the establishment of his capital, thenceforth called by the Turks Istanbul, was to re-people the city. Many who had fled were promised protection of property and religion, but thousands were deported to Adrianople, Gallipoli and Anatolia. On the other hand thousands were brought to Constantinople from Serbia, Albania and Greece, and many more arrived from all parts as slaves, immigrants, prisoners of war and refugees. The largest settlements were those of Anatolian Turks who were brought into the city to stabilise it, and these were settled in districts many of which were given the name of the town or village from which they had come.

Mehmed was extremely far-sighted in matter of state-craft and he adopted the principle, which had been practised both by the Byzantines and the Arab Caliphs, of allowing the various religious communities to be governed in the first instance by their own leaders. He selected an eminent Greek clergyman to be patriarch of the Greek community, exempted the clergy from taxes, allowed the Church full autonomy of administration and free religious practice. In Byzantium all authority among the Greek Orthodox had lain with the Emperor, and the patriarch lived in the shadow of the imperial palace. This imperial tradition was all ready to be taken over by the Turks. Mehmed also let the Chief Rabbi continue to order the civil and religious affairs of the Jewish communities.

The conquests continued. Bosnia, Herzegovina and Albania were added to the Turkish possessions and by 1460 all Greece had fallen. The Crimea and Rumania were added and eventually the Sultan Selim I conquered Syria and Egypt. Between 1520 and 1566 his son Suleyman the Magnificent (who was a contemporary of Charles I, Francis I, Henry VIII, Elizabeth I, Leo XX, Columbus, Cortez, Raleigh and Drake) added Belgrade, Rhodes, Hungary, parts of Mesopotamia and Armenia, the Yemen, Aden and the coast of North Africa. As it has been said: 'He had gifted advisers whom he was strong enough to control and wise enough to use', and it is in his golden age that we like to picture Ottoman Turkey. Indeed, the rest of this book will in the main be describing Ottoman life in this period, since it was then at its richest and most secure. Suleyman's reign was, however, a watershed and with its end began the slow decline of the Ottoman Empire. It was Suleyman who granted the first Capitulations, that is, permission to let foreigners be ruled by their own laws within the empire. Capitulations were originally granted to trading companies, later to the government of any state whose subjects had sufficiently important interests within the Ottoman dominions. Under the Capitulations foreigners were not subject to Turkish law and paid no taxes; their houses and places of business were inviolable and they could be arrested and deported only by their own ambassadors. Disputes among themselves were settled by their own consular courts according to the laws of their own country, and non-Muslim Turkish subjects in foreign employ could be given this privileged status by a consular diploma. Abuse of these privileges was rare in the early days, since the foreign communities were small and mainly mercantile, but by the mid-nineteenth century these Capitulations were taken as a sign of Turkish weakness.

It may seem surprising that the empire could go on declining for nearly four centuries. The reasons for this are partly that the Sultans tolerated a very low degree of political unity and a great diversity of social and religious practice, and partly because of the internal weaknesses, external pre-occupations and mutual jealousies of the adversaries of the Ottoman Empire. However, it was impossible for control over such widespread and heterogeneous dominions to be uniform, and local autonomy began to increase at the outside edges. But the greatest reason for the decline was that the empire was primarily a military machine. With Suleyman the Sultan ceased to be a ghazi and became an emperor. Sultans only exceptionally led their armies into battle, accompanied by their ministers, and the army entered on an era when there were few wars except defensive ones and therefore no new slaves and rich booty. For a time the empire enjoyed the fruits of its ancestors' conquests, and then the weaknesses began to reveal themselves. The army became obstinate and unmanageable, and although there were some attempts at reform on western lines all efforts proved inadequate to fight the entrenched old order. The ulema had also arrogated great power to themselves and were almost as anarchic as the Janissary troops. High office could be bought, and even in the great cities learning and ability were not necessarily qualifications for judgeships, and the medreses—religious schools—were totally ignorant of the world outside. Meanwhile the imperial house was also suffering degeneracy and corruption.

It had taken twelve years of warfare with his brothers before Mehmed I could feel secure on his throne. Murad II had to contend with rival claimants to the sultanate in the persons of his uncle and younger brother. Mehmed II was moved by the experiences of his father and grandfather to insert a spine-chilling clause into his 'Code of Laws of the House of Osman', between two prosaic regulations concerning respectively the officers who were to carry the petty cash when the Sultan went on campaign and the quarterly issue of new clothing to the Palace page-boys:

> On whichever of my sons God confers the Sultanate, it is proper that his brothers, for the sake of the order of the world, be slain. Most of

the Ulema have declared it permissible. Let them act accordingly.

In the seventeenth century this Law of Fratricide was abandoned and instead the Sultan's brothers were confined in gilded imprisonment within the Palace. The intrigues of the Sultans' concubines to secure the succession, each for her own son, were a further source of weakness within the dynasty. Small wonder that so many of the later Sultans were men of little moral fibre and scant knowledge of the world. Yet nevertheless they remained the pivot of the empire and held its destiny in their hands.

In the administration, candidates began to buy office so that promotion was more often a matter of money than of merit, and those who could buy their positions often displaced loyal slaves. Tax collection gave way to tax farming, with all the extortion and corruption that this implies. The empire's trade and industry remained backward compared with the level of industrialisation and mechanisation of the western powers. This was reflected in its army supplies, ship-building and training. Because of the traditional contempt for the west, based on its earlier centuries of supremacy, the Ottoman Empire long refused to adopt the new weapons and tactics, and it was possibly this smugness of the Muslims in the face of infidel inventions that left them unable to deal adequately with the revolts in their Balkan territories, and from the last quarter of the seventeenth century the balance of power in eastern Europe inclined against the Turks. In 1774, by the Treaty of Kuchuk Kaynarja, the Russians gained not only territory but also the right to navigate the Black Sea, the Bosphorus and the Dardanelles. The landing of a powerful Russian force on the Asian shores of the Bosphorus was concluded by the Treaty of Hunkar Iskelesi in July 1833, which gave Russian shipping freedom of the Bosphorus and the Dardanelles and denied this right to other powers except with Russian approval. In addition the Russians also gained the right to 'remonstrate' with the Sultan in favour of Moldavia and Wallachia and to make representations on behalf of a new Greek church to be built in Constantinople. This marked the breakdown of Turkish dominance in the Black Sea, and also over their Christian subjects, for it gave the Russians an excuse to claim to be protectors of all subjects of the Turkish Empire who were members of the Greek Church.

In the eighteenth century Turkish power also receded in North Africa. The Sultans ceased to send pashas to Algiers, Tunis and Tripoli and allowed the title to be assumed by hereditary local rulers. In Egypt the authority passed to the Mamelukes, and by the end of the nineteenth century Turkey had become the 'sick man' of the history books.

At its greatest the lands of the Empire had stretched from Budapest on the Danube to Aswan on the Nile, and from the Euphrates almost to Gibraltar. It comprised in Europe: the Balkan Peninsula, Transylvania, Moldavia, Wallachia, most of Hungary, Podolia, the entire north coast of the Black Sea, Crete, Cyprus and the Aegean Isles; in Asia: Asia Minor, Armenia, most of the Caucasus, the valleys of the Tigris and the Euphrates as far as the Persian Gulf, the whole eastern Mediterranean coast and a strip along the Arabian peninsula to the Gulf of Aden; in Africa: Egypt, Tripoli, Tunisia and Algeria. The population of the Empire numbered some 50 million, including, of Muslims: the Turks, Tatars, Arabs, Kurds, Turcomans, Berbers and Circassians; of apostates: numbers of Bosnians, Albanians and Bulgarians; of the Christian Churches, mainly Orthodox: the Greeks, Hungarians, Serbians, Rumanians, Armenians, Georgians and Egyptian Copts. There were also Jews and, in addition, slaves captured from among the Germans, Poles, Russians, Greeks, Italians, French and Spaniards.

It would be beyond the scope of this book to depict the variety of conditions in such an Empire over a period of 600 years, but the peculiar stability of Ottoman society and the consequently slow rate of change and decay make it possible to describe a way of life which continued, in part or whole, for a very considerable period.

It is necessary to consider here the connotations of the words 'Turk' and 'Ottoman'. In this book the word 'Turkish' is used in the general western sense, which makes no distinction between Istanbul and the rest of the country, but delimits Turkey from her empire, though in fact no such geographical entity as Turkey existed in the Ottoman scheme. There were certain dominantly Turkish-speaking lands, roughly corresponding to the territories of the original Ottoman conquests in Rumelia and Anatolia, but these were divided into administrative areas under the central government in Istanbul in the same way as most other lands held under the Sultan. The concept of Turkishness in the national sense simply did not exist, neither did the term 'Turkish Empire': it was know as the 'High State', or the 'Guarded Dominions', or the 'Abode of the Faith'. For that matter, even the term 'Sultan' was a western adoption; the sovereign was known in his lands as the Padishah—a Persian word meaning emperor. 'Turk' was used to mean peasant or yokel; it described the Turkish-speaking people of Anatolia. The ruling class, which is to say the sovereign and the establishment, thought of themselves as Ottomans and Muslims, and, although there was religious solidarity, this literate urban governing class considered the people they called Turks as country bumpkins and creatures of coarser clay. With the exception of men of religion, and of a few of remarkable military or administrative ability who rose to positions of authority and literacy, every ethnic Turk remained fixed in his place in the rigid social system. It was, however, in his terms, a solid self-respecting place, supported and protected by the system.

The Ottomans had inherited a hybrid language consisting of Turkish with a high proportion of Persian and Arabic borrowings, a combination which made for great richness and majesty, and the speech of the Turkish population was dismissed by these Ottoman-speakers as 'crude'. They themselves used Ottoman as the language of administration, Arabic as the language of religion and Persian as the language of literary culture, especially poetry. Only at home, in unguarded moments, and perhaps to servants, did they speak the Turkish which was the language of the population of Anatolia.

2

The Establishment

It is fortunate that, given the size and variety of their conquests, the Ottomans revealed an extraordinary talent for administration, and indeed it is this, rather than the sheer extent of their acquisition, that marked the peculiar greatness of the Ottoman Empire and stamped its particular quality on the life of its subjects. The Ottoman genius lay in the combination of a superbly well-trained civil service, a system of justice based on the sacred laws of Islam and therefore bound to command pious respect, and a ferocious, loyal and disciplined army, all tempered by a certain flexibility when confronted with local customs so deep-seated that it would have been dangerous or impossible to override them. To this was added considerable imaginative and common-sense humanity, which reconciled many conquered Christian territories to their lot. Indeed, although the majority populations of many of the provinces differed entirely in race and religion from the Ottomans who governed them, there was extraordinarily little civil disturbance, even when in times of war the policing forces of the government were removed to fight elsewhere, leaving a handful of administrators in charge of the subject people. Within the framework of local conditions, and allowing for the intransigence and lawlessness of certain tribes, the inhabitants of Muslim lands, steeped in traditions of obedience and resistance to change, were also incorporated without much difficulty into the system. It was the interplay of many factors that, from inception through flowering and into decline, kept the empire a force for 600 years, with, at its head, the constant symbol of its might and magnificence, the supreme ruler, the Sultan.

Although the dynasty lasted as long as the empire, the succession did not automatically pass to the eldest son. At the age of fourteen or thereabouts, after the ceremony of circumcision, the young princes were sent out to govern various provinces of Anatolia, where their abilities and progress were reported upon. Eventually the reigning Sultan would decide which son should be his heir and he would be appointed to a

2 *The accession of Sultan Bayezid II in 1481*

strategic post near the capital. To avoid the rise of opposing factions
supporting other claimants to the throne it became the practice, as we
have seen, to put to death the other brothers (and their sons), and they
were strangled with a silken bowstring—the form of execution reserved
for those whose noble blood it was impious to shed. This barbaric necessity was held to be a small price to pay for the avoidance of dynastic wars
and civil strife: 'The death of a prince is less regrettable than the loss of
a province.'

The death of the Sultan himself was not accorded undue mourning,
and his harem was quickly hustled away to the Old Palace and his
favourites dispersed. The new Sultan took office immediately, sitting on

his throne before the Gate of Felicity in the
New Palace which Mehmed Fatih, the
Conqueror, had built on the headland
facing the entrance to the Bosphorus. There
he received the homage of the court; the
notables of his kingdom kissed the hem of
his robe and swore their loyalty. This was
followed by a ceremonial assembly of his
Council—the Divan—when the new min-

*3 Akche (actual size) of
Suleyman I dated 926 (AD
1520) minted at Janja, in
Bosnia. This silver coin was the
unit of currency*

isterial appointments were announced and gifts were distributed. At
this Divan the formal orders were given for the minting of the new
coinage which was to bear the new Sultan's name, his titles and the date
of his accession. Each Sultan had a distinctive tughra, which was used
as both signature and royal cypher. It took the form of an intricate
monogram of his name, the letters arranged in decorative form. These
tughras were used on documents, imperial decrees, and wherever the
royal seal was needed and, later, on coins. Between five and fifteen days
after came the Girding, a ceremony of some mystique, conducted in
greater privacy. The Sultan would make the journey by barge up the
Golden Horn to the tomb of Eyyub, a companion of the Prophet
Muhammad who died in battle and was buried where he fell and whose
mausoleum there was the holiest Muslim place in Europe. There, in the
presence of the Chief Mufti representing the spiritual powers and the
Chief Sword-Bearer representing the imperial household, and some few
other dignitaries temporarily in the ascendant, such as the heads of
certain dervish orders, the hallowed swords—for there were sometimes
more than one—which had been brought from the Treasury, were
solemnly girded about him. After this ceremony the Sultan rode on
horseback into Istanbul, visiting the tombs of the great Sultans on his
way back to the palace.

Word was sent to all parts of his dominions and to all the other great
rulers that a new Sultan had come to power, and he received such
magnificent gifts that many foreign Ambassadors and envoys in Istanbul
who saw the splendour of some of the presents were seriously embarrassed
by the inadequacy of their resources and the impossibility of their offering
a worthy gift, and wrote home in shame and despair of the camel-loads
of treasure from Russia and China and India that passed through the
streets of the city.

On his accession the Sultan became an absolute despot, head of a
system of government based on the Sacred Law of Islam. This, while
exerting its own rigid limitations on his powers, nevertheless invested
him with enormous authority as its head and chief officer, particularly
since as heir to the Caliphate—the office of Successor of the Prophet—he
was also technically the political and military chief of the Muslim community. In order to be sure, however, that all his political decisions were

4 The Sultan returning to Istanbul through the streets of Eyub

rightly guided, he would obtain the approval of the Chief Mufti—the senior religious dignitary—for the execution of any important political act. If, as sometimes happened, the Mufti withheld approval, the Sultan would abandon the project or, if he was strong and determined, have the Mufti removed from office and replaced with one sufficiently co-operative to find some religious justification for the Sultan's proposal. A weak and unpopular sovereign, on the other hand, might find that a formidable mufti, backed by a rebellious people, would denounce him as unfit to administer the divine law, and he would be deposed in favour of another member of his family more deserving of the honour. Generally, however, the Sultans held the reins of power with a firm hand, and in this their chief advantage was that the Administration, and in part the army, were in fact their slaves over whom they had power of life and death. This came about in the following way.

The number of slaves born within the domain of Islam steadily dimin-ished as masters, in order to win merit in the eyes of God, granted them their freedom, or because the children of slave mothers and their Muslim masters automatically had free status. This meant that supplies had constantly to be replenished either by capture or by purchase from territories outside. Of the booty of war one-fifth went to the Sultan; consequently this proportion of all the captives seized in the wars against the infidels became slaves of the Sultan, and of these those suitable became soldiers. With a lull in the conquests in Europe, however, the flow of Christian captives came to an end, and as it was forbidden by the Holy Law to enslave a fellow-Muslim the Asiatic conquests brought no new recruits. And so an entirely original idea was conceived: at irregular intervals, as the demand dictated, a levy was made from among the unmarried male children, aged generally between ten and twenty years, of the Christian population of the Sultan's dominions, largely from the Balkans. On the occasion of a levy a Janissary officer and his clerk, furnished with a letter of identification from the Chief of the Janissaries, a warrant of authorisation and a supply of uniforms, travelled round his assigned area in the Christian provinces, such as those of Rumelia, Albania, Greece and Serbia. Criers summoned the children, who came with their fathers and the village priests bearing the baptismal registers. Under the supervision of the local judge and feudal overlords the recruiting officers selected the most suitable children, that is, those of fine physique and attractive appearance, good moral calibre, who knew no Turkish and had no trade, were not married and had had no experience of city life, and were not orphans who had had to fend for themselves. Only Christian children, and in addition those of one particular group— the Muslim Bosniaks—were chosen, and they had to be unspoilt, unsophisticated raw material which could be moulded to fulfil the destiny that was planned for them. Although only sons, who would eventually be their parents' sole support, were not taken there was, inevitably, much hardship as well as anguish occasioned by this heartless system, and it caused many an early peasant marriage which would thus exempt the groom. Nevertheless their subsequent training culminated in opportunities of such extraordinary advancement that many families were resigned or even happy to see their boys go, and as many bribes were offered for the inclusion of non-Christian boys in the levy as to buy off Christian children; the Muslim children from Bosnia, being already circumcised, were particularly carefully guarded on their way to the capital to prevent Turkish boys from being smuggled into their ranks. To prevent abuses two registers of names, parentages, age and description were made by the clerk who accompanied the officer; one copy remained with the recruiting officer and one accompanied the drover who herded the children to Istanbul. This levy of boys was known as the Devshirme—the Collecting.

On their arrival at the city the boys were formally admitted to Islam, that is, they raised their right hands and recited the Profession of Faith: 'I hereby testify that there is no god but God; Muhammad is the Prophet of God', and were then circumcised. The more intelligent and promising boys were then selected to be taken into the Palace Service; the rest were hired out into Turkish families in Asia Minor and Rumelia to work on the land and learn Turkish and to become thoroughly Islamicised, and then, as vacancies occurred, they were drafted into the Janissary Corps of the army, or to some other service. In either capacity they remained slaves of the Sultan all their lives, obedient to his whims and commands,

obliged to go wherever he sent them, to accept whatever position or duty
was allotted them, and to submit to death at his command at any time
in their careers. On the other hand, particularly in the Palace Service,
there were no limits to the authority and wealth to which they could
aspire except those set by their own ability and loyalty, and the title of
Sultan's slave was an honourable one. Completely cut off from their
earlier lives, and subjected to a rigorous and absorbing training, they
became both entirely dependent on the Sultan and competent to fulfil
the requirements of his service, and so well were they chosen and prepared for their tasks that many of these sons of ignorant illiterate peasants
became men of education, culture and extraordinary ability, on whose
administrative skill depended the organisation of an enormous and
complex empire.

On selection for Palace Service the handsomest and most intelligent
youths were sent to the Palace as pages, under the control of the Chief
White Eunuch; others went to one or other of the old imperial palaces
in Bursa and Edirne, or to the special palace schools in Galata and
Istanbul. They were well cared-for but in conditions of simplicity and
discipline, with great insistence on obedience and good manners. Punishment was strict but not immoderate: ten strokes on the soles of the feet
with a thin cane, not more than once a day, was the maximum inflicted.
While carrying out comparatively menial tasks as pages in the royal
household they also underwent a most thorough education in Turkish,
reading Arabic as the language of the Koran, and Persian as the
language of poetry and literature, as well as in history, law and religion.
As a kind of precaution against possible later unemployment, or perhaps
as part of a tradition which even Sultans shared, each boy was also
taught some sort of craft or trade. In addition they were trained in the
use of arms, horsemanship and military strategy, and at all stages their
progress was reported upon by their supervisor, the eunuch who watched
over his group of ten pages day and night. They were promoted according to merit through the various grades of palace service; the most able
and meritorious became the Sultan's personal attendants until, at the
age of twenty-five, they were considered ready for the world outside.
Those of the top rank went to appointments as governors of provincial
towns; some became members of the Noble Guard, a crack corps with
special duties, but most went into service with the regular cavalry—the
Sipahis of the Porte. The Sultan himself was present at the great farewell
ceremony and congratulated each man on his new position; he gave each
an embroidered coat, a beautiful horse and sometimes gifts of money.

Those who went into the administrative service, and who proved by
their devotion and capacities to be worthy of higher office, were rewarded
with steady promotion until the best of them returned to the Palace to
the positions of highest responsibility. Even there the training process

continued, since the Privy Council itself was a kind of school in which the members profited from the teaching and examples of their seniors, discussed and shared their ideas and demonstrated their fitness for further promotion, even to be the very head of the Service, the Grand Vizier himself. He was the Sultan's representative and Chief Minister, who was responsible for all the appointments in the army and in both the central and provincial administration, who commanded the army in time of war if the Sultan chose not to do so himself, and who was responsible for the preservation of law and order in the capital; his official residence, known as the Babiali, or High Gate, which Europeans rendered more picturesquely the Sublime Porte, was synonymous in western eyes with the Ottoman government. Yet he was as much the Sultan's slave as the lowliest new recruit, as liable to summary execution if he lost the Sultan's confidence, or to deposition if he proved inadequate or no longer suitable.

Parallel with the administrative service, and as exclusively in the hands of the free-born Muslims as the former was in those of foreign-born slaves of Christian origin, was the legal system and the religious hierarchy in which its authority was manifested. The legal obligations of the empire derived from four sources: the Sharia, the Sacred Law of Islam which was greater than the Sultan and which he was powerless to change; the Kanuns, which were written decrees of the Sultans; Adet, which was the established custom, especially powerful in those remote and wild districts where the unwritten laws had for centuries provided the only rough justice; and Urf, which represented the sovereign will of the reigning Sultan and, when expressed in writing, became itself Kanun, overruling any previous Kanuns and any Adet which ran counter to it.

The Sharia was, of course, of paramount importance, influencing as it did not only the legal and religious but also the social, ethical and economic life of the people. It was the province of the ulema, that is, the religious functionaries of all grades, from the humblest village school-master to the learned men who, having pursued a clearly-defined course of study and training, became the established heads of law and religion. They began their higher education in the medreses, colleges attached to the larger mosques, in which were taught such studies as grammar, logic, metaphysics, geometry and astronomy. Beyond these, the higher medreses, of which there were twelve grades, taught those sciences concerned with the Koran and Sharia, including law, theology, exegesis and jurisprudence. When the students had completed their training they became eligible for appointment to the office of cadi—judge—in one of the provinces. The more ambitious began at the bottom of the list of the twelve higher medreses, this time as teachers, and ascended through them in the order of their importance, thus acquiring qualification for higher office. When they had taught their way through nine of them, concluding at one of the great schools attached to the Suleymaniye mosque in Istanbul, the highest category of appointments was available to them. They could, in order of increasing importance, become teachers in the top three medreses, or cadis of any of the fourteen most important towns in the empire, with Mecca and Medina at the head of the list, or Cadi of Istanbul itself. Above that in rank lay the office of Cadi-asker of Anatolia, that is, Judge of the Army of the Asiatic provinces, and higher yet that of Cadi-asker of Rumelia, Judge of the Army of Europe.

The most important post of all, and the head both of the strictly religious functionaries and of the judiciary, and so symbolising the inseparability of these two aspects of the Holy Word, was that of the Mufti of Istanbul, who bore the title Sheikh-ul-Islam. He was usually promoted from the rank of cadi-asker, and was of paramount importance in the structure of the empire, although he had no temporal authority and played very little active part in affairs. His, however, was the responsibility for deciding that a war on which the state proposed to embark was holy, for proclaiming it so and for sending out word that it was incumbent on Muslims to fight in it. He was also consulted on whether any Kanun which the Sultan wished to promulgate was in conformity with the Sacred Law, of which he was the guardian and chief interpreter; he was the keeper of the Sultan's conscience. The Sheikh-ul-Islam was the spiritual counterpart of the Grand Vizier, and neither had precedence over the other, although the Sheikh did not sit in the Sultan's Divan, where the forces of religious law were represented by the Cadi-askers of Rumelia and Anatolia. Other high religious dignitaries included the Sultan's own hoja—teacher—who had tutored him before his accession and was naturally accorded great reverence, the two imams who led the prayers in the Palace chapel or whichever mosque the Sultan elected to attend on Friday, the Head Physician of the Palace, a man with terrifying responsibilities, and the Head Astrologer whose chief duty lay in drawing up the charts and calendars from which could be ascertained the propitious moments for actions and events.

All the ulema were paid out of religious endowments, whose revenues were received, administered and invested by a special Treasury department, and this income was supplemented by various fees and fines. The ulema were not subjected to taxation, nor could their property be confiscated and, unlike that of the Sultan's slaves, it could be inherited intact. In addition they were the administrators of justice, and this combination of privileges and authority brought them great prestige as well as great wealth.

The judiciary itself was divided into cadis and muftis. The cadis, or judges, on whose integrity, skill and good sense Ottoman justice depended, were nominated to posts in Europe, North Africa and the Crimea by the Cadi-asker of Rumelia; those for Asia and Egypt were nominated by the Cadi-asker of Anatolia, and the two services remained independent. On his appointment each cadi appointed one or two na'ibs, or deputies, to assist him. In addition to the settling of disputes, the cadis drew up civil contracts, did all the notarial work of the district, administered the property of orphans and minors, acted as registrars and officiated at important weddings. In addition, cadis as well as muftis might be consulted for technical advice by the senior administrative officer of the district.

In dealing with legal cases the cadi had recourse first to the teachings of the Sacred Law, for guidance on the interpretation of which he might ask the advice of a mufti; he then considered the Sultan's Kanuns, which were the regulations governing secular criminal law and procedure not covered by the Sharia, and which prescribed the relevant fines and punishments. Not surprisingly, perhaps, the Kanuns were in general harsher than the Sharia, prescribing severer penalties for more offences more summarily, although they had all been approved by the ulema before they were issued. They were, very sensibly, framed in clear vernacular Turkish and distributed to all courts in every town; orders were given to make the contents of each decree known to the people; they were read out aloud in public places and every man had the right to ask at any government office or law court for an official copy of the code of laws, for which he paid a small fee.

Finally, the cadi would consult the customs and immunities which obtained in the region, and employ his experience and good sense in arriving at his decision. Although the Fetwas—legal opinions—of great muftis were recorded and circulated for study, no written records were kept of past cases and there was no reference to precedent in matters under dispute. The decision of the court—which was final, admitting of no appeal since all courts were considered equal—was rendered briefly and with little delay.

The muftis, or jurisconsults, varied greatly in their training. The Sheikh-ul-Islam was responsible for the appointment of muftis to the chief cities of the empire, where one was assigned to each cadi to act as his associate. These had usually spent some years teaching in one of the lesser medreses. The muftis of the smaller provincial towns had usually had little or no preparation for office, while those in the villages were often some local religious official, possibly the imam or the school-teacher, or even simply a wise old man, owing his title to the acclamation of the villagers. When a cadi or a private citizen had a legal problem which required recourse to the Sacred Law he would propound it to a mufti, whose responsibility it was to recast the question in hypothetical form, using certain fictitious names for the protagonists, such as Zeyd and Amr and Bekir for men, and Hind and Zeyneb for women. He might, in important matters of state, incorporate the relevant citations from the

Koran, Tradition, and the manuals of the Hanafi school of law. The answer, called the Fetwa, would generally be terse, often a simple 'Yes' or 'No', conventionally accompanied by a saving 'God knows best'. The following are typical examples:

> Question: If, while Zeyd and Amr are wrestling, Zeyd picks Amr up and hurls him to the ground and Amr's left arm is broken and becomes totally useless, what is incumbent on Zeyd?
> Answer: Half the blood-price (i.e. the financial compensation for homicide) is incumbent.
> Question: Zeyd and Amr are captains. While they are sailing one dark night they fail to see one another and their ships collide and both are sunk. If Bekir, who is on Zeyd's ship, should drown, are his heirs able to say to Amr: 'Bekir drowned because of a collision with your ship' and take the blood-price from Amr?
> Answer: No.

Sometimes, on the other hand, the Fetwa was more detailed and exposed a reasoned argument, backed by scriptural texts. In the great cities the mufti's office would consist of several sections, devoted variously to the receipt of questions, their formulation after reference to the relevant books, delivery of the Fetwa and investigation of problems from the cadi's court. The Fetwa was generally final and settled the matter under dispute; thus the many private citizens who sought and received them, paying a fee for the service, were able to go to court prepared with a mufti's ruling. This, together with the accessibility of Kanuns, meant that every man could discover his legal situation, and ensured a considerable degree of justice. It meant, also, that many cases never needed to reach the cadi's court at all, and the affair was settled privately. This happened frequently in other circumstances. For example, each social group, whether town guild or village council, had its own organisation which arbitrated in internal disputes and whose Sheikh administered summary justice. Then again, in those parts of the empire where the school of law locally adhered to differed from the Hanafi school favoured by the Ottomans, the population would naturally prefer to submit its problems to the local mufti, with his homely wisdom and understanding of local conditions. Finally, there were certain offences against the conventions which were always punished without referring the case to the intervention of a judge, and this was especially true among nomad groups, who imposed the death penalty immediately in cases of adultery or unchastity or as reprisal in a blood feud.

Those criminals, however, who had been found guilty in the cadi's court could be subjected to a variety of punishments; physical, ranging from death to cutting off the hand, flogging or stoning; imprisonment or exile; monetary fines; official admonition by the cadi, and several others besides. The treatment of minors and insane or imbecile people, however, was extremely humane, and they were held to have no criminal responsibility. The swift and sometimes severe punishments, the efficiency of the police and the collective responsibility of the social groups for crimes committed in their midst, contributed to the very considerable observance of the law and the extraordinarily low crime rate. It is possible that the humbler subjects of the empire enjoyed more dependable, albeit harsh, justice than those in high office. When the Sultan's Divan functioned as a law court for the trial of capital cases of such officials, it was usually without the knowledge of the offender. If he was found guilty an usher was sent with the court's decision and an order of death, which was given to the nearest official with power to put it into execution. The condemned man hurriedly settled his worldly affairs and made his peace with God, and was then quickly dispatched and his head cut off and brought back to the Sultan by the waiting usher, as proof that the deed had really been done. It has been said that as many as forty heads had been known to arrive at the court of Suleyman the Magnificent in the course of a single day.

5 *The first lines of a firman, bearing the tughra of Suleyman I*

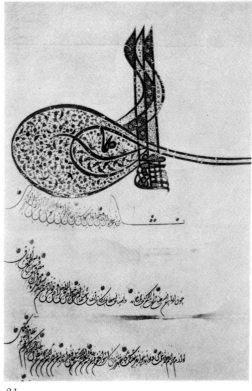

Another method for securing the redress of wrongs was to submit a petition to the Sultan, in the hope of securing a firman, a royal decree, in favour of the petitioner. The petitions and reports of matters to be brought to the attention of the sovereign were read out at the imperial Divan, and, if necessary, oral representations were also heard; matters of lesser importance were heard at the Grand Vizier's Divan. When, after discussion, a decision had been arrived at it was noted down by a junior official and served as the basis for the phrasing of the decree which was subsequently issued. Sometimes these were completed and sent to the petitioner immediately, especially in cases where a Grand Vizier or some other high official was empowered to make a decision without consultation, but generally the draft of the decree was prepared, examined and corrected by a senior official, or even, if it were very important, by the Sultan himself. These decrees, whether in fact issued by the Sultan or not, were written in direct speech as though in the Sultan's own words. They usually began with an exposition of the situation in need of redress, which was followed by the Sultan's decision, sometimes including his reaction to the situation and a reminder of what was proper or customary: finally came an exhortation underlining the importance of the matter and bearing instructions that the order was to be carried out without delay and a report on progress quickly made. A threat of punishment for violation of these instructions was also generally included. A fair copy was then drawn up and the imperial cypher, the tughra, fixed at the top, and the document sent to the addressee. The cypher was usually applied after the draft had been written, but when the Sultan was away with his court at Edirne, or had gone to war, blank pages with the tughra already affixed were deposited with the Vizier who had been left in charge of the city of Istanbul, so that decrees could be issued without delay. The gist of each decree was copied into an official register in extremely concise and businesslike form.

Not all decrees dealt with the redress of private wrongs, and in military or administrative matters, such as the maintenance of public security, the suppression of revolts, the recruiting, mobilising and deploying of troops, the granting of fiefs or the appointment and control of officials, decrees were addressed to the Governor-General of the province or the Governor of a district. Fiscal matters, especially those concerned with government expenditure, were addressed to the Treasurer of the district or province, while those requiring executive power and a knowledge of law—for example, the capture, trial and punishment of rebels and other criminals, or the status and places of worship of non-Muslims—were directed to the Governor and Judge of the district. Others might be sent to muftis, military commanders, or whichever officials were appropriate and responsible, all, on receipt of the document, being bound to put the instructions into immediate execution. A request for the investigation of the surreptitious fixing of pipes and taps to divert public water for private consumption was sent to the Superintendant of Waterways and the Cadi of Istanbul; a command to warn off the poachers who had been stealing the exclusively royal fish from the waters near Bursa was sent to the Cadi of that town, and to the Cadi of Istanbul a complaint about the requisitioning for postal couriers of the horses and mules belonging to guests of a khan, thereby scaring off customers with consequent loss of revenue, concluding 'This must stop!'; to the Governor-General of Egypt went a decree ordering him to supply 150 porters to carry stone and wood to mend an aqueduct damaged by the floods of 1564.

Eventually, with the passing of time, there came a falling-off in all aspects of justice. Orders were disobeyed, and judges began to line their pockets, imposing harsher fines and accepting bribes. Severe penalties began to be imposed as horrid warnings rather than in the measure of the crime. Rowers were needed for the galleys and many criminals for whom other penalties should properly have been prescribed were sent to the ships, as were some of the wilder element in the lawless provinces who had as yet committed no crime punishable in the Sharia. But when, in its inevitable decay, the system showed signs of oppression and injustice it was due to a decline in the quality of the administration rather than to faults in the laws themselves; the institutions of justice remained one of the glories of the empire.

There was an Arabic saying, which was believed to have come from the Prophet himself: 'God Almighty says "I have an army which I have named the Turks. Whenever I am wroth with a people I unleash the Turks upon them".' This reputation of the Turkish army, the right arm of the Sultan, reposed for centuries on the traditions of absolute fearlessness and unquestioning obedience, and these qualities were shared indivisibly by what might have been expected to be the two utterly dissimilar branches: the feudal land-owning forces of Muslim freemen, and the slave corps of Christian-born Janissaries. The feudal forces consisted principally of knights and cavalrymen—Siphahis—who had been granted fiefs of land, which were worked by peasants over whom they had seigneurial rights, and from which they collected the revenues. In return they had to serve in the army, either in rotation or when summoned for campaign, and according to their rank and the size of their holding they had to provide one or more equipped and mounted men-at-arms who accompanied them on their period of service. In peace-time some of these were employed on police duties. None of these soldiers had any regular training, but they were reared in the tradition of arms, horsemanship and bravery. Their holding of land was generally conferred on their sons; even if the boy was a minor he would take possession and send a man-at-arms to represent him until he was old enough to fight. Sometimes further awards of land were made for conspicuous bravery or long faithful service; sometimes the land-holders were deprived either temporarily or permanently of part of their holding if their conduct merited the punishment. Some of the land was held not for the benefit of individual soldiers but to provide revenues for such particular purposes as the maintenance and supplying of fortresses and garrisons. In time of war one Sipahi in ten was allowed to stay behind to maintain order in the countryside, and while on campaign those on duty were allowed to return home while their division was laid up in winter quarters, so that they could collect their tithes and dues from the peasants, because the yield from the land was their only source of income and they had to maintain themselves both in peace and war.

There were in addition askeris, soldiers who had a smaller grant of land which they worked themselves; of these, only one out of a team of four or five was called at a time and the others contributed to his support while he was on duty. These askeris paid no taxes and were usually employed in ancillary services. The nomad peoples of the countryside — the Yuruks — paid pastoral dues and were engaged, with the askeris, on the building of roads, digging of trenches, the transport of arms and provisions and the casting of cannon balls. There were also a certain number of volunteers who served with the feudal forces, some of whom fought simply for loot, but there were also some Christian renegades who, having become Muslim, fought and rose in the ranks until their ability and ruthlessness towards the Christendom they had abandoned brought them to high positions. No fewer than twelve great generals, and the four most famous admirals in the history of the empire, had been renegade Christian soldiers in an army which took little account of a man's birth and provided limitless opportunities for his advancement by merit.

The other branch of the army, the Janissaries, was made up from the youths who, recruited in the Devshirme, had been found in physique and aptitude to be more suited to soldiering. From their service with Turkish families working for the feudal landlords in Anatolia, they were brought back to Istanbul and examined for their fitness to pass to other duties. Some were drafted into branches of the imperial service — into the Company of Gardeners or Tent-pitchers or some other department whose name equally belied the scope of its activities. Others went into the corps of Armourers which was stationed both in the capital and the provinces and whose tasks were to manufacture and repair arms and ammunition, and to guard all army transport and stores on campaign; others were gun-carriage drivers or gunners, whose chief officer commanded the arsenal and the great powder magazines. Some promising young men went into the Admiralty; others who had done less well were hired out as labourers to anyone who would employ them. But by far the greatest number joined the formidable Corps of Janissaries, the paid soldiers who were the Sultan's most powerful single weapon. The Corps was headed by the Agha of the Janissaries who was also Chief of Police in Istanbul and sat with the ministers at the Divan. In war he accompanied the Sultan and commanded his troops. In the administration of his men he was assisted by a council of his five most senior officers. The Janissary army was made up of a number of divisions and each of these had its own barracks or, in time of war, large tent, which bore its distinguishing symbol for all to see: a key, or an anchor, or a fish, or a flag. Some men even had the sign of their division tattooed on their arms or legs. These barracks, containing storerooms, kitchens and sleeping quarters and staffed with officers, a clerk and chaplain, were the only homes these soldiers knew, and their lives were entirely bound up with their unit. Cut off in childhood from their families, forbidden to marry, not allowed — and, indeed, without any skills — to engage in trade, their lives were made up of fighting in wartime and the preservation of order in peacetime. They were able with all weapons and particularly skilled at archery, and later with small arms; they were always extremely handy with the crooked dagger that each man carried at his belt.

The ceremony of enrolment into the Corps was an occasion of great honour to the initiates. The new boys who had been assigned were lined up and, at a signal, ran to Company Headquarters, where the first to arrive was accounted the senior man of his year's intake. After the evening prayer they were formally admitted: the non-commissioned officers placed a turban on each man's head and a rough cloak round him, and he went to kiss the hand of the lieutenant in charge of his barrack-room, who welcomed him with the appellation 'yoldash' — 'fellow-wayfarer'. If there was a hasty admission in time of war the ceremony was somewhat curtailed: the recruits passed before the Agha of the Janissaries and the Sergeant-major wrote down each man's name, slapped him on the back of the neck and said: 'Off you go to Company number . . .'. Greater than their loyalty to the Sultan was their loyalty to their comrades, and members of the same barrack-room had the greatest claim of all by an oath sworn on a tray holding salt, a copy of the Koran and a sword. Even more revered than the standards of their Companies were the huge copper cauldrons of which each barrack-room had two or three, in which their ration of rice was cooked and around which they sat in the evenings. If one of these were ever lost in battle all the officers of the barrack-room were dismissed with ignominy and never again accepted into the same Company, if they were re-accepted into the army at all. As usual, the titles bore little relation to their duties: all the officers with the exception of the standard-bearer had names connected with the provision of food. The senior commanders were the Soup-men, the next two officers were the Cook and Head Scullion: below them were Barrack-room Chief, Quartermaster, Watercarrier and Black Scullion, and they were promoted through these ranks by seniority of service. As the numbers of Janissaries increased they eventually became more unruly and rebellious; when they refused to drink the soup that was provided for them after Divan guard duty in the Palace, and kicked over the cauldrons, the authorities knew that they were sulking and sought to appease them before they made their displeasure felt. They insisted on approving the accession of each Sultan, and when Bayezid II in 1481 bought their support for his disputed claim to the throne the Janissaries treated the 'gift' as a precedent and exacted it from subsequent Sultans under threat of withholding their approval.

6 *Janissary uniforms. The soldier second from the left is wearing the typical headdress*

So greatly were they feared that their mutinies always concluded with the redress of their grievances.

The Janissary uniform was particularly distinguished by its headdress because it was traditionally believed that the first group of Christian levies had been sent to Hajji Bektash, the founder of the Bektashi order of dervishes, for his blessing. As he laid his hand on their heads his sleeve fell against them, and their hats thereafter carried a long flap of cloth in imitation of this sleeve. Those Janissaries who had volunteered for some particularly dangerous mission and survived it were entitled to wear another distinctive sort of cap which proclaimed their exceptional bravery, and provided an additional reason for swagger. When a group of these arrogant powerful ruffians demanded not only food and drink but also 'tooth rent'—money in compensation for the wear on their teeth while eating the food—the unfortunate civilian providers of it could hardly be expected to put up much resistance. It was probably more as a gesture of solidarity than from any strong sense of identification with them that the Sultan Suleyman himself was nominally enrolled in the first regiment of Janissaries, and collected a soldier's pay with the rest of the men from his colonel on pay-day.

The Bektashi dervishes, whose links with the Janissaries were rooted in those apocryphal early days, became so closely connected with the Corps that in 1591 the Order was actually affiliated to the 99th Division, and its Sheikh was given the rank of Soup-man; eight dervishes were attached to the Company's barracks in Istanbul with the task of praying for the empire and its armies, and marching in front of the Agha of the Janissaries on parades and formal occasions, all dressed in green, while their leader called: 'Allah Kerim'—'God is Bountiful'—and the others replied with a long-drawn-out, sonorous 'Huuuuuuuu'—'He'.

Since the Janissaries were devoted exclusively to fighting and police work, a number of artisans attached themselves to the Corps to satisfy their needs, and among the guilds they represented were cobblers and barbers, saddlers and bow-makers, coppersmiths and tinsmiths, candle-makers and sword-smiths and slipper-makers and sellers of cooked sheeps' heads and countless others besides. Many of these were employed and paid by the state, and on declaration of war a senior Janissary officer chose a number of artisans to accompany the troops and provide necessary goods and services.

The armies of both the feudal soldiers and the Janissaries were famous even among their enemies for the perfect discipline and superb order that ruled in their camps. As soon as the horsetail standards were planted on the plains of Davudpasha or at Uskudar, signifying the intention to campaign in Europe or in Asia, and therefore the call to arms, the Turks 'came together for war as though they had been invited to a wedding', but to their joy in battle they brought an orderliness and abstemiousness in their life in camp, a system for the immediate establishment of good conditions for soldiers and animals, that was their pride and a great part of their strength. A body of water-carriers as well as medical orderlies accompanied the soldiers both on the march and in the field, and nothing was left undone which could contribute to their well-being and morale. For this was a professional army, and from the early days of the empire until well into the sixteenth century their campaigns were annual. The Sultan, having appointed a Kaymakam, Lieutenant Governor, to administer the city in his absence, would leave Istanbul and, accompanied by his Chief Vizier and court, ride out at the head of his soldiers. The usual plan was to set out in the late autumn so as to be installed in winter quarters within striking distance of the target. The spring battles would be followed by mopping-up operations and a straggling return home in time for the summer and the first harvests. The most usual weapons for man-to-man fighting were the single-edged sabres which curved to a point, the broad curved scimitar, the short yataghan like the sabre but smaller and with the edge on the inside curve of the blade, rapiers and daggers. In addition, hanging from either side of the saddle-bow, the cavalry carried hatchets and maces; subsequently rifles, pistols and carbines were added to the armoury.

The navy, although a force to be reckoned with in the period of its greatness, was an altogether less coherent organisation. In the earlier days of the empire the chief occupation of the Sultan's maritime territories was some trade and a great deal of piracy, particularly against infidel ships, and when, as so many contemporary rulers had done, the Sultan decided that the country needed a fleet of ships and had them built at his own expense, this kind of privateering experience became the best possible preparation for service in the navy. The conquest of Istanbul and the subjugation of the lands round the Black Sea made it unnecessary to do much more than police those waters, which freed the navy for service in the Aegean and Mediterranean, and it so increased in skill and power that in 1522 it was able to drive the Knights of St John out of the island of Rhodes, from which base they had for years been raiding Ottoman ships and even small coastal towns. At about this time, too, the great corsair Barbarossa began his successful forays, in the course of one of which he found somewhat to his own surprise that he had seized Algiers. He asked the Sultan for his help, which came, together with the title of Beylerbey—Governor-General—of the Province of Algiers, which thus took it neatly out of Barbarossa's hands and added it to the Sultan's territories. Two more North African provinces were soon added: Tunis and Tripoli, and eventually Cyprus was captured. Meanwhile other Ottoman warships were making conquests in the Indian Ocean, acquiring the greater part of Yemen, although their strength in those waters proved inferior to that of the Portuguese navy which was also taking and consolidating possessions in that area.

In 1533 Barbarossa was called to Istanbul to supervise the construction of larger boats in the huge new shipyards there, and to organise the navy. Early the following year he was created Lord High Admiral and was also given the feudality of the Aegean and Mediterranean, which thereafter provided naval Sipahis and, later, supplied and maintained a warship.

The ships, for which the Turks adopted Italian names, from that great seafaring nation the Genoese, were sometimes galleons or galleass, which might be of some 1,500 to 2,000 tons. These were very high fore and aft, and carried heavy cannon projecting through portholes on the upper and lower decks. In addition to masts and sails there were tiers of oars, each of which required several men. More commonly used, however, were galleys which also possessed sails, but these were seldom used in time of war. The galleys were long, narrow and light, and lay very low in the water. One large gun pointed forward from the bow, and two or four were mounted on a platform amidships. The rowers, chained by one leg, sat usually three men to an oar, with twenty-six oars on each side of the ship; a taskmaster with a whip kept the top rank under his eye and set the time for the stroke. In battle these rowers could manoeuvre the ship so that its sharp beaked prow could ram other craft, or they could turn it so that their sailors could climb over the side and board the vessel they were attacking. They were too light and too low to ride safely in bad weather or rough seas, but they were perfect for negotiating shallow tricky water or for penetrating inlets and rivers. Many towns which thought themselves safely situated on the edge of bays too shallow to permit the passage of a warship, and which had not observed the black-painted enemy lying flat on the water during the hours of daylight, were surprised by a sudden attack in the middle of the night by marauders who looted and destroyed and set out to sea again before they could summon the help of their own soldiers.

The ability of some of the greatest sea-captains was not, however, supported by efficient sailors. Because of the nature of the warfare many rowing and fighting men were required, and those available were always found to be unsatisfactory. The work of rowing was harsh and thankless, and the only regular supply came from the criminal class who had been condemned to it as a form of penal servitude; these were supplemented by prisoners of war, especially those seized from rival ships. The fighting men were drawn from various sources, and were never suitable. At first, Greek, Albanian and Dalmatian sailors were used, but they proved unreliable; then irregular troops and Turkish nomads were tried, but they were unable to adapt themselves to life at sea and besides became easily corrupted by the possibilities of looting and pillage. Eventually companies of Janissaries or of Sipahis drawn from the Admiral's feudal holding were employed, although they never achieved the degree of organisation and dependability of the land forces. The greatest lack of all was felt in the sphere of true seamen, those experts in weather and navigation, the handling of compasses and the reading of stars, and the interpretation of shoals and currents. Numbers of ships put to sea with a totally inexperienced crew, and when, in the years of decline, the office of Admiral became a perquisite of the Court and both he and his officers began to supplement their income by the sale of commissions, the navy was scarcely fit to put to sea at all, and the fleet's annual summer cruise became an occasion of mockery as well as of dread in the ports and islands which it visited.

These years of decline, which overtook both the Palace Service and the army, did not, of course, come suddenly. The decay in the splendid old systems which probably began when the Sultan became the settled monarch of a comparatively stable organisation, even before the empire was at its territorial greatest, took hold almost imperceptibly and progressed so slowly that to summarise it in a few lines is to telescope a process that took almost 400 years. But inevitably, with the gradual abolition of the Devshirme, the Palace schools began to take well-born children or sons of retired Palace officials, even orphans and poor children who seemed promising. These were all free-born Muslims, and so without the total dedication to the service of the Sultan that had distinguished their predecessors. The Janissaries were always defiant and troublesome in the cities although brave and loyal in battle; their discipline was also weakened by the loss of Devshirme recruits, and as Turks became permitted to enrol in the Corps, and permission to marry provided both distractions from a soldierly career and the necessity to supplement their pay with some craft or trade, and since many turbulent elements were also enrolled with the idea of keeping them out of mischief, the once-proud brotherhood degenerated into a slovenly band whose sole link with the army was their pay-books, which they even sold or gave as security against loans, thus providing some extremely unpleasant surprises for the authorities at any time of mobilisation.

A factor in the stability of the empire which demonstrated both the humane flexibility and the practical good sense of the Ottoman administration was the status of the non-Muslim subject peoples, that is, the Christians and Jews. Under the principle 'The bended head is not to be stricken off' all Muslims were bound to spare the Peoples of the Book, members of those monotheistic religions which had preceded Islam, provided that they agreed to pay a poll-tax and gave no trouble. Certain rules of behaviour were laid down for them, mainly designed to prevent provocative or offensive behaviour towards Muslims and to ensure prompt payment of all dues; in return their lives, property and religious freedom were guaranteed. These religious communities, known as millets, were accorded a surprising degree of autonomy in the conduct of their affairs, being left under the supervision of their own leaders who administered their own laws, since the Sharia would not be expected to apply to them, except where they came into conflict with a Muslim, in which case the cadi applied Islamic law. The leaders of the communities were responsible to the Turkish government for the good order of their members and for the collection of their taxes. At the head of the Orthodox Christian Church was the Patriarch, who for ceremonial purposes had the Turkish rank of a pasha of three horsetails, and whose dominion over his flock included a court of law and a prison in Istanbul. The Jews, who were much in demand for the provision of doctors and interpreters and scholars of various kinds, were organised under their Chief Rabbi; they and the Armenians—a label which included all small groups from miscellaneous Christian sects—were exempted from the Devshirme which was the only consistent intrusion by the Turks into the lives of the millets. The authorities sometimes intervened, however, to protect the communities themselves from the excesses of an unjust leader; occasionally, too, they found it necessary to remind some members of the millets of their subordinate position, although this was usually done to placate some jealous or critical section of the Muslim community rather than in a spirit of persecution. Generally, the millets' affairs were left in the hands of the people who understood them best—their own leaders—and this lenience was amply repaid in co-operation and docility.

3

Religion and Superstition

The religion of the Turks was Islam, which they acquired during their progress westwards across Arab lands. To become a Muslim, that is, a follower of Islam, needed only a profession of faith in the formula 'I testify that there is no god but Allah; Muhammad is the Prophet of Allah.' To remain in the Faith required adherence to four additional practices: observance of the five daily prayers, the giving of alms to the poor, fasting in the holy month and making, if possible, the pilgrimage to the holy city of Mecca, in Arabia. However, although in essence Islam is a simple religion, in which there is no apostolic succession and any man can be the imam, or prayer-leader, and no priesthood since no man can come between God and worshipper, a tremendous body of religious practice circumscribed Muslim life and governed its thinking.

The sacred book of Islam is the Koran which was revealed to Muhammad (A.D. 570–632) and this, together with the collections of Hadith, or traditions, that had been codified in the ninth century, formed the basis of Muslim law. From these religious sources—for the Hadith were held to represent the Prophet's point of view on a wide variety of questions—the lawyers and religious leaders could by analogy or precedent, or sometimes quite imaginative interpretations, find a ruling applicable to any legal or social or religious problem put before them, according to the principles of whichever of the four great schools they followed. Thus the laws and customs that grew up about the religion came to constitute a rigorously defined and all-embracing way of life, so that a Muslim knew or could find out at all times and in any circumstances what fell into the categories 'forbidden, disapproved, permitted, recommended, obligatory'.

By the sixteenth century, therefore, the basic requirements of Islam had accumulated an enormous number of formulae which dictated all details of their performance. The five daily prayers could be said anywhere, with the exception of the noon prayer on Friday for which attendance in a congregation was obligatory: large numbers of men, however,

7   *Friday noon prayer in the mosque of Sultan Ahmed*

went to a mosque, either the small local mesjid, or a great jami. This was basically a large, usually domed, hall, big enough to hold the entire congregation of the quarter for the noon-day Friday prayer. In the centre of one wall was an empty niche, the mihrab, marking the direction of Mecca, and on the right was the minber, or pulpit. Since the form of prayer required a number of prostrations on the ground there were no seats. Attached to each mosque were one or more minarets, slim towers girdled with balconies which were reached by an inner staircase. In the courtyard of the mosque was a fountain, usually a large tank of water encased in marble with spouts from which the water flowed.

The religious functionaries of the mosque consisted of the imam, who was the unofficial chief of the local Muslim community and whose duty it was to lead the Friday prayer; the va'iz, who preached the homily; the hafiz, who recited from the sacred book; the khatib, who delivered the Friday sermon and led the invocation of God's protection on the Sultan and his family; and the muezzin, who was responsible for crying the ezan, or call to prayer, out over the rooftops for all the community to hear. In a small mosque these functions might be combined in one person.

Five times a day, at daybreak, just after noon, midway between noon and nightfall, just after sunset and after nightfall, the muezzin climbed the stairs of the minaret and gave the call to prayer from the galleries four times, facing the points of the compass, using the formula: 'God is most great. I testify that there is no god but Allah. I testify that Muhammad is the Prophet of Allah. Come to prayer. Come to salvation. There is no god but Allah', and adding, for the dawn prayer, 'Prayer is better than sleep'. On hearing the call the faithful stopped what they were doing, or rose from their beds, and unless they chose to pray at home went to the fountain of the mosque. There they performed a ritual ablution, washing the face, mouth, nose, ears, neck, hands, forearms and feet. The worshipper then proceeded to the door of the mosque where he removed his shoes and either left them outside—few crimes were considered so despicable as stealing shoes from outside a mosque—or, laying them carefully together, sole to sole, placed them in a rack inside the door. Then, taking up his position facing Mecca, he made the necessary preliminary declaration of intention to pray, and began the recital, in Arabic, and the extremely formalised movements of head, hands and body which accompanied it. Only three very slight irregularities, such as coughing or a very small clumsiness, were allowed; in excess of this the prayers had to be recommenced and completed in perfect devotion. For certain prayers a rosary of ninety-nine beads, originally used for telling the ninety-nine names of God, was passed through the fingers. Women were not allowed to pray with the congregation, but were segregated either in galleries or behind partitions, and in all cases hidden from the gaze of men.

After prayer the most important duty of the Muslim was the giving of alms. An amount was exacted based on a man's possessions in excess of what he needed to pay his debts and maintain himself and his household, which included houses, furniture, clothing, slaves, such articles as armour and weapons, or the books and implements of scholars and doctors, or the tools of a workman's craft. It varied in proportion between about a fifth and a fortieth, depending on such considerations as whether the property consisted of fruits of the earth, or animals living on forage, or gold and silver or merchandise. In addition to this levy the generosity of all Muslims was encouraged, and the money was used for the relief of the indigent, to ransom slaves and to free debtors, to support holy men, succour travellers, finance holy wars, and to remunerate the alms-collectors.

The duty of fasting also took on rigid forms. The sacred month of Ramadan began officially with the first sight of the new moon, and the evidence of any Muslim in the neighbourhood that he had seen it was enough for the proclamation of the month of fasting. Thereafter for twenty-nine days all Muslims over the age of puberty, and in good health, were obliged to fast throughout the day, from early light—'the time when a man can distinguish a white thread from a black thread'—until sunset. The prohibition included eating, drinking, even the unintentional swallowing of spittle, smoking and any sort of pleasurable occupation. Since the Muslim year was lunar the months moved through the seasons, and when Ramadan fell in the hot summer the faithful suffered severely from lack of water.

The performance of the pilgrimage was incumbent on every Muslim at least once in his life unless he was too poor or too ill, although it was possible for one who was unable to go to send in his place a man whose journey he financed and who promised to dedicate the pilgrimage to his sponsor's intention. Sometimes, too, wealthy men contributed to the expenses of poorer pilgrims, thereby associating themselves spiritually as well as financially with the holy journey. The pilgrimage required the presence of the pilgrim in Mecca at the beginning of the twelfth month, and the journey was begun with a great celebration some time before, the date of departure depending on the distance of the starting-places from Mecca. The travellers would have to pass over wild, lonely territories and through the lands of brigand tribes who 'having sown neither millet nor wheat, awaited the passage of the pilgrims to reap a rich harvest'; for safety and convenience, therefore, they travelled in bands, joining up with other groups and the great caravans from Egypt, Syria, Iraq and the Yemen, until the converging streams became a mighty river that paused for a moment on the heights overlooking the holy city, then flooded down into the valley in which it lay.

Having arrived safely near the goal of his hazardous journey, the

44

8 The Kaaba at Mecca

pilgrim bathed and prayed and then assumed his special dress, the ihram, which consisted of two simple pieces of seamless cotton, linen or wool with no ornamentation; one of these was wrapped round the loins, the other thrown over the left shoulder and passed under the right armpit. The feet had to be uncovered at heel and instep and the head was bare. Women were wrapped in undyed cloth, the face heavily covered. The pilgrim then turned to Mecca, made the declaration of intent—which preceded all religious performance—and descended into the city, reciting and singing. His first visit was to the Kaaba, a large roughly cube-shaped building which according to one tradition was erected by Adam on a spot on earth exactly below an identical building in heaven; another tradition had it that it was created by Allah, who built Mecca around it, then encircled the city with holy ground, and finally created the rest of the world around that. The Kaaba was covered with a rich black cloth ornamented with gold bands and heavily embroidered with verses from the Koran. Set in the south-east corner near the door was the Black Stone, probably an aerolite, which had been a cult-object in pre-Islamic times but was now considered to be God's eye on earth, and His hand which blessed all who touched it. The pilgrim entered the precinct of the Kaaba with the right foot and advanced and kissed the Black Stone. He then passed seven times round the Kaaba in an anti-clockwise direction, pausing each time to kiss the Stone again. Several other rites were performed at Mecca, some of very ancient origin but incorporated into Muslim religious performance, including a visit to the well of Zemzem which stood in the courtyard of the mosque and whose acrid waters had miraculous properties. The pilgrim then made the six hours' journey to Mount Arafat, for the obligatory atten-dance at the sermon which was given in the afternoon of the ninth day of the month and was the most solemn requirement of the pilgrimage. He then proceeded to Mina where, again carrying out a very old pagan rite, he threw seven pebbles at each of three pillars, one of which was called the Great Devil.

The culminating ceremony was that of sacrifice, in which the beast— sheep or goat or cow or camel, according to what the pilgrim could afford—was placed facing Mecca with its forelegs tied; its throat was then cut, or, in the case of a camel, stabbed. Although this was not a religious requirement it was an integral part of the ceremony and on that date, the tenth day of the twelfth month, known as Kurban Bayram, the sacrifice of an animal, even only a hen if the celebrant could afford no more, took place not only on the pilgrimage but throughout the Islamic world. These rites concluded, the pilgrim had his head shaved and resumed normal dress and indeed normal life, for the period of the pilgrimage had required rigorous abstention from all pleasures. His reward came, however, in the absolution of all his sins, obtained by his presence at Arafat, the satisfaction of a religious obligation faithfully performed, in the warmth and solidarity experienced in the sharing of this performance with co-religionists of all nationalities from all corners of Islam—a solidarity not without its unifying political force—and finally, on his return, in the pride of his right to wear the green turban which signified that he was a hajji, a pilgrim. For although the pilgrimage was enjoined on all Muslims, comparatively few undertook the difficult and dangerous journey, and a safe return was cause for rejoicing and reflected glory on the whole community.

These five requirements, the 'pillars of Islam', were considerably com-plicated and embellished in the public imagination by the accretion of a host of popular beliefs, which added colour and humanity and a comfortable supernatural shiver to the sometimes austere rigidity of the formal religion. The principles of the Muslim faith were expressed in the two articles of the Profession, but the believers peopled the world with spirits. In the highest rank were the angels who carried God's commands; Gabriel brought the revelation of the Koran to Muhammad himself. Between angels and men in unearthly powers, yet lower in creation than either, were the jinns, who were created out of fire and could assume any shape or be invisible. They could eat and drink and love like humans, and even eventually die. Some were true believers, but others, the sheytans, were infidels led by the devil Iblis who was, like Lucifer, a fallen angel. These evil jinns engaged in a variety of troublesome activities, from mischievous displacement of objects to demoniac possession requiring exorcism to drive them out. Charms were recited and amulets worn to keep them away, and they had a particular dread of iron, so great, in fact, that it was enough to say the word loudly to frighten away any lurking imp whose presence was suspected.

Many popular beliefs were associated with death, for Muslims believed in the immortality of the soul, resurrection and judgement, and rewards in paradise or punishments in hell. When the last footsteps of the burial party had died away, two terrible angels, Munkar and Nekir, were believed to appear at the sepulchre and the body, temporarily reunited with his soul, sat up and answered their questions on his faith. If they were not satisfied with the results of this examination they tortured him; if they were convinced that he had been sufficiently devout he was allowed to sleep until the last day. On that day all would assemble for judgement, and when their good and evil deeds had been weighed they would pass over the bridge called Sirat, 'finer than a hair and sharper than a sword', that extends over the middle of hell and leads to paradise. The blessed would cross easily, riding on the rams that they had sacrificed in their lives on Kurban Bayram; the wicked would slip and fall into the bottomless pit of boiling pitch. Since they were Muslims, God in His goodness would eventually release them, but those of other religions would be condemned to hell for ever. Infant children would pass straight over without having to give an account of themselves and so would martyrs, that is, any unpaid soldier who had been killed in battle in defence of the faith, any man who had innocently met his death at the hands of another, any victim of dysentery or the plague, provided that he had not sought to evade it, or anyone drowned or killed by the fall of a building. In paradise there was only happiness and ease and, as well as every gratification of the senses, Muslim men and women in paradise received the supreme reward of seeing God face to face.

It was believed possible for a Christian to become converted to Islam after death, and for a Muslim who had been buried among infidels to risk losing his faith in their company; to bury these properly God had provided 72,000 camels who continually moved about transporting all such bodies to Muslim tombs.

Intercession could be achieved by prayer, especially the recital of the Fatiha: 'In the name of God, the Merciful, the Compassionate. Praise is to God, the Lord of the Worlds, Master of the day of judgement. Thee do we worship and Thee do we ask for aid. Guide us to the straight path, the path of those to whom Thou hast been gracious, not those who have been visited with wrath nor those who go astray'; by the lighting of candles on a saint's tomb or by adding to or repairing the tomb building, or by establishing a foundation for perpetual prayers and Koran readings; and by sacrifice, for the success of which blood had to be shed. Besides those of Kurban Bayram, sacrifices were offered at the initiation or on the termination of any dangerous business such as a war or a journey, and at such critical moments of life as a circumcision, or a bride's entry into her new home. They were offered for a life spared from accident or sickness, for escape from danger, in times of illness, fire or pestilence, after ominous dreams, on the erection of a new building, at coronations and in honour of important visitors, in crisis and in thanks.

There was, however, another religious force in the life of the people: the dervish orders. Most of them had originated in the twelfth and thirteenth centuries, inspired by mystics who wanted to approach God more closely and who formed brotherhoods for the propagation of what they called Muhammad's 'secret teachings'—since they had to lend them authority —as distinct from those in the Hadith which were available to all Muslims. These teachings became formulae for the organisation and rites of the various orders, and the bleak impersonality of pure Islam, with its simple doctrine of submission to a remote and arbitrary Deity, encouraged membership of these close and companionable religious fraternities. Functioning as a combination of sect, club and secret society, they attracted enormous numbers of adherents, particularly from among the poorer classes; indeed, many guilds of craftsmen had among their patron saints some holy member of a dervish order, and their popularity made them so powerful that they have been described as 'a religion within a religion and a State within a State.'

The obligations of membership were, above all, obedience to the Sheikh, or head of the order, followed by vows of secrecy and solidarity, attendance at meetings and contributions to the upkeep of the order, and the living of a pious life; the social and spiritual advantages received in return were sufficient to make some of these orders so strong that they became potentially important allies or, more often, dangerous enemies of both the civil government and the formal religious establishment. It has been estimated that perhaps as many as 10% of Muslims had some association with a dervish sect, although the concentration was far higher in the towns. Of the 200 or so orders which had, at their height, headquarters in Istanbul as well as in Mecca and Medina, among the chief were the Kadiri, whose tolerance and excellent sermons persuaded many Christians and Jews to embrace Islam; the Rifai whose adherents were able, when in a state of trance, to walk on live coals and swallow serpents and pierce and lacerate themselves without apparent hurt, the touch of their Sheikh's spittle closing all wounds; the Kalenderi, who wandered about as barefoot mendicant pilgrims with no possessions; and the Mevlevi, the most aristocratic and intellectual of the orders, who arrived at a state of ecstasy by whirling to the music of pipes and drums and who had such respect and authority that their representative was sometimes privileged to be present at the Girding of the new Sultan. But the most popular of all among the Turks was the Bektashi, a turbulent cheerful order which incorporated many heterodox elements, rendering it attractive to both Christian and Muslim. In its rites the drinking of wine or spirits, forbidden in Islam, was permitted, and women participated, unveiled, on terms of absolute equality. Initiates belonged to a tekke, or lodge, in the privacy of which took place not only religious ceremonies but also social gatherings of great conviviality and freedom which were much criticised by outsiders for their moral laxity. The order was, however, extremely widespread and its influence was as profound in all walks of artisan life as it was in the famous Corps of Janissaries.

All holy men and wandering dervishes were treated with reverence, not only by the superstitious public but also, as a matter of policy and in deference to popular sentiment, by the Sultan himself. They were admitted even into the Divan, and their blessing and advice, which was sought by all outside, was there freely given and listened to. During Ramadan and other holy days they entered any house at will and were made traditionally welcome.

Yet another and older force in the life of the simpler people was that of popular religion, which had its origins in instincts and impulses so primitive that many places of pilgrimage and veneration, holy from the earliest times, continued to be visited by both Christians and Muslims. Some of these sites had a natural feature—a mountain peak, or tree, or unusual rock, or spring; some were man-made, such as columns or carved stones or tumuli; what they had in common with the third and largest group—tombs—was that they were all identified with the grave of some miracle-working saint whose haunt they had become. Some of these graves belonged to Jewish prophets such as Noah or Joshua or Daniel, some to Koranic saints such as Khidr or the Seven Sleepers, some to old tribal gods and some to founders of religious orders, and the multiplicity of tombs ascribed to each did not detract from their supposed authenticity. There were in addition the graves of many holy men, a category which included preachers, teachers, hermits who had lived lonely contemplative lives, warriors who had died for the Faith, dervishes who had inspired troops in battle and performed supernatural feats of arms with wooden swords or simply with the power of their spirit, and others who had lived in union with the world of nature, so that wild deer came to them to be milked or even offered themselves to be sacrificed.

Association with the miracle-worker for the purpose of winning his intercession and so gaining a wish was achieved in various ways: the lighting of candles, the driving of nails, the knotting of rags to nearby trees or window-bars, the rubbing of stones, the eating or drinking of earth or water from the holy site. Direct contact or absorption was most efficacious, but any object which had been in physical contact with the grave shared its magic power, and guardians of the shrines earned their living from the gifts of money made by people who left small objects in them overnight to acquire that power, or by supervising incubation in holy caves and bathing in holy water, or by selling little cakes of earth which were eaten to cure epilepsy or paralysis or malaria. Some pilgrims supplicated for employment, or a good harvest, or a house, or any other object of their desire: at the tomb of Koyun Dede lamp-oil was given, and as long as it burned the donor's child would be good; at the tomb of Helvaji Baba barren women unwound cotton and laid it out in great loops as they prayed for the gift of a child, at the same time pledging a quantity of the sweetmeat helva if they were to get their wish. The helva brought in fulfilment of their vow by those happy women whose wish had already been granted was distributed among the other supplicants, and was considered to have special powers. The requests for supernatural aid were accompanied not only by money for the custodian but also by gifts to the holy place of such things as brooms, oil, candles, embroidered handkerchiefs, prayer mats and Korans. The custodian himself was nearly always a dervish of one of the orders.

The sanctity of the Greek ayazmas—holy wells—almost always ante-dated their Christian attributions and they continued to attract simple people of all religions; many Christian shrines and even country chapels and churches became places of Muslim veneration, the original saints to whom they were dedicated becoming characters of Muslim legend, for although in the Greek Church sacred places had to be associated with a saint in the official church calendar, or be consecrated by a bishop or patriarch as the grave of a neo-martyr, in Islam any tomb could be declared holy by popular acclaim, provided that there had been a miracle.

In addition to the graves of Muslim saints and the sacred sites inherited from Christian and pre-Christian times, many more sprang up in com-memoration of nameless holy men known only as baba—father—or dede —grandfather,—but in all cases the inviolability of the precincts was so universally respected that some of the humbler class left their possessions there for safe-keeping, and it was no uncommon sight to see a ramshackle collection of bundles and sacks and cooking-pots lying unheeded in some neglected corner of a village shrine.

Certain Christian customs were adopted, too, 'in case they were useful or had some good in them.' Before taking a sea voyage in the early part

CHANG

06/16/15

TIFFANY L

31111012769020

p11541933

Hold Slip Horizontal

9 *The Church of St. Sophia in Istanbul, used as a mosque. Many of the Christians'*
superstitious practices associated with miracle-working stones and pillars were adopted
by the Muslim worshippers

of the year the Turks of Istanbul would send to enquire whether the
Orthodox priest had yet given the spring blessing to the waters; some
Muslims had their children baptised, not for the good of their souls but
to bring bodily cleanliness, the rite being considered particularly effective against leprosy. Some went so far as to believe that a Christian holy
relic would protect them in battle against Christian arms, but generally
the forces of pure Christianity, as distinct from popular practices often
common to both religions, were looked on as hostile and capable of
unleashing supernatural forces which might need to be fought or neutral-
ised or conciliated. After the Conquest at least one church in each town
was turned into a mosque, and whenever, through what the local
Christians would call a miracle and the Muslims black magic, the
building underwent some catastrophe—if a newly and perhaps hastily
built minaret fell or was struck by lightning, or if the muezzin died, or
evil spirits had been seen—the building was usually either closed altogether or put to secular use. Crucifixes could be extremely dangerous
and were generally broken not out of malice but to rob them of their
hostile powers; religious statues too could be the abode of devils and
sources of harm unless they were mutilated, and the eyes of the painted
figures on church walls were scratched out not in a spirit of vandalism
but in self-defence.

51

10 Talisman for protection against cholera, wounding, and pestilence, to be wrapped in waterproof cloth and hung round the neck

Many beliefs that had once had some origin in religion were expanded into far-reaching superstitions. Writing of any kind, originally revered by the illiterate because it might be the Koran or was at any rate in the same script as the Book, became a charm of the greatest magic. The best talisman of all was a copy of the Koran; sometimes a small one was worn in an embroidered leather or velvet case carried on a silk cord which passed over the left shoulder and across the body; very powerful too were the ninety-nine names of God. But many other written charms included the names of saints and angels, or magic squares, or diagrams and combinations of numerals, and sometimes the words of an incantation were interpolated between the verses of the Fatiha. These were worn by adults and children, hung on cradles and round the necks or on the foreheads of animals, and suspended in houses and shops; in fact they were used everywhere as protection from evil. In addition, these written charms were used in combination with various incantations and procedures for exorcism and for the procuring of aid from all manner of unknown powers. As love-charms they could, for example, be rolled up and used as a wick in an oil lamp, burning in the room of the beloved, or folded and inserted into an onion which was slowly roasted on the hearth until the cold heart burned with passion, or they could be hidden in thresholds or beds or clothes. Others could be used to cool off the affection of one no longer loved, or to separate two who had fallen in love. They could bring back a loved one from a distance, or a runaway slave; they could prevent a man from talking, or sleeping, or beating his wife or children; they could find lost objects and expose thieves; they could cure all manner of sickness. The proper use of these charms was in the hands of the wise men and women, of which every community possessed at least one, a feared but essential element in society, who would be consulted on the choice of propitious times and suitable matches and who made up spells and antidotes.

There were many other forms of charm: water from the holy well of Zemzem, pieces of black brocade from the covering of the Kaaba, and cakes made of dust from the tomb of the Prophet and stamped with an invocation, which as well as being worn or hung as an amulet could be mixed with water and drunk. No building would have been considered safe unless it bore an inscription in tiles or sculpture which read: 'Ya Allah. Ya Hafiz'—'O God, O Protector'—and all medicines were vastly increased in efficacy if they were administered in suitably inscribed bowls and cups.

Greater than any specific ills, however, and responsible for most of them, was the Evil Eye which, it was said, 'emptied palaces and filled graves', and it was as protection from this that most charms were devised. It would be impossible to over-estimate the power of the Eye and the degree to which it affected thought and speech. Since any possession, however mean, or any attribute, however mediocre, might attract the notice of someone less fortunate, none could consider himself safe from it, and as its maleficence was inspired by envy it was necessary to conceal or underrate anything which might attract its baneful influence, and use all means to avert it. For this reason it was out of pure consideration that a beautiful baby or precious possession was admired with no expression of open praise, but in the most circumspect terms, usually in some such indirect way as with the exclamation 'Mashallah'—'Whatever God wishes'—implying that His power extended even to the creation of this marvel. Indeed, the generosity of those who warmly pressed an object on one who admired it was often based on the feeling that with that admiration the Eye had been put upon it and the owner would thenceforth have no good of it.

Since they were uncommon in those parts, blue eyes were considered to be particularly dangerous, and for this reason the Franks—the general term for all Europeans—were thought to have powerful and unlucky eyes. The best antidote was a blue eye which would cast

11 Charms against the evil eye.
(a) Horns of a stag-beetle, with blue glass 'eye' bead and a coin
(b) Silver filigree amulet containing a verse of the Koran and hung with a cowrie shell, a wolf's tooth and a shrivelled chestnut

back the evil influence, and so one of the most popular of all charms was made in the likeness of a blue glass ball, sometimes with a yellow and black eye on it. This charm could be anything from a small blue glass bead, which could be pinned to a baby's dress, to an elaborate jewel as large as a hen's egg, set in gold. By extension, the shape, if not the colour, was used in the form of carved or ornamented balls which were hung in the gateways of buildings, or set into the outside walls. Even the enemy's cannon-balls could be used for this purpose, and would indeed in some mysterious way have double strength. Ostrich eggs which had been brought back from the pilgrimage were very effective indeed, but whatever the form of protection continual vigilance was necessary.

There were hundreds of other smaller superstitions that pervaded and sometimes bedevilled everyday life; as in all places at all times, many of these were devoutly held only by the most credulous, preserved as entertaining customs by others, and dismissed with scorn as mumbo-jumbo by the logical and stout-hearted.

4

Portrait of a City

The city *par excellence* was Istanbul. When, in the winter of 1457–8, the Sultan moved the seat of government from Edirne to the new capital, it became the political and cultural heart of an empire whose expansion served to heighten the city's prestige and magnificence. All that was finest, richest and most varied was to be found in Istanbul, and any appointment to another town, even in the capacity of governor of a province, was felt to be a little exile. Since, however, those raised to positions of responsibility in the provinces, whether in the Administration or the Judiciary, had all been trained within the imperial household or in the great religious establishments of Istanbul, the life they had known there became the model for that of all the notables of the empire, and even, by imitation, for those of humbler origin as far as means and etiquette permitted. The administrators and officers who had been trained in the tradition were imbued with its spirit and influences, and on appointment outside they took with them the ideals of many of the private and public features of life in the capital. In addition, of course, the old capitals of Bursa and Edirne had always been centres of authority, wealth and culture; Izmir was the most famous of the 260 ports in Ottoman lands and the biggest commercial centre in Asia Minor, while those large Anatolian cities to which the princelings were sent during their period of training acquired as a consequence a high standard of amenities. All cities, therefore, although in varying degrees smaller, less rich and less varied, possessed some of the characteristics of life in Istanbul. The towns or quarters predominantly Christian were preserved undamaged, but adapted as far as possible according to the Turkish town-planning system, by which provision was made for wells and canals, market gardens, flower-gardens and vineyards, town walls with fortifications if necessary, and the development of any resources that the town possessed.

The strategic position of Istanbul itself was unrivalled, for it stood at the gateway between the Black Sea and the Aegean, and was the bridge

12 Map of Istanbul in 1572 according to a Western traveller, largely drawn from an earlier map of Byzantium

uniting Europe with Asia. Into the Black Sea flowed those major waterways the Danube, the Dniester, the Bug, the Dnieper and the Don, giving access to the Balkans and Eastern Europe as well as to South Russia: possession of its southern shores gave control of the Tigris and Euphrates, and, with the Caspian Sea, access to the Volga as well as a route to the Oxus and eventually the Indus. The Aegean, and thence the Mediterranean, opened the way to Greece, Europe and Africa. Overland, the great trade-routes of east and west converged upon the city: Brussels, Zanzibar, Kiev, Samarkand—any centre of population with something to sell lay on a road to Istanbul. It was perhaps this cosmopolitan character which distinguished it, apart from its political and administrative importance as the centre of government, from the other cities of the empire. In addition to the foreign element of traders, artisans and travellers drawn to the city by its wealth and fame and the opportunities it offered, there were the Christians and Jews left over from Byzantine times or expressly brought in to settle in the town during exchanges of population, as well as the foreign ambassadors and their entourages; indeed, the suburb of Galata which lay on the eastern side of the Golden Horn remained predominantly Frankish in character, and there and in Pera lived most of the Venetian, French, English and Genoese who had settled as merchants or practised a profession—the French surgeons were esteemed particularly skilful. In 1477, almost a quarter of a century after the Conquest, the population of Istanbul was reckoned to be between 60,000 and 70,000, of which about three-fifths were Turkish.

In the following contemporary list the figures are of houses, each reckoned to contain four or five people:

9,753 Turkish
3,743 Greek Christian
1,647 Jewish
818 Armenian Christian
267 Crimean Christian
31 Muslim Gipsy

There were in addition 3,667 shops, all, as was the custom of the time, uninhabited. A hundred years later the total population had grown to about 500,000 of which 58% was Muslim and 42% infidel, that is to say Christian and Jewish.

Although it stood a little apart from the rest of the city, the focus of life in Istanbul was the Palace of the Sultan, the Serai, which included within its walls the centre of government, the court and the royal household. It consisted of a number of gated and guarded precincts, each with groups of pavilions and one- or two-storey buildings set among courtyards and gardens, the whole covering an enormous area and surrounded by a high wall.

57

Near the entrance to the Palace was the Janissary Court, through which passed thousands of people of all ranks on their way to attend the Divan or to see the Sultan. Here too passed trains of camels bringing arms, provisions of food for the Palace, and the riches collected by the tax-gatherers on the way to the imperial coffers. Here stood a huge tree under which were two small columns, used for the execution of those who had been sentenced to decapitation, and as a grim reminder of the fate of the Sultan's enemies corpses were exposed to passers-by, sometimes, as a sign of particular contempt, with the victim's head placed between his feet.

This courtyard led into the precinct which contained the offices and official rooms in which the councils of state were held, the imperial Divans which met every Saturday, Sunday, Monday and Tuesday. As the Sultan passed on his way to the Divan the humbler petitioners lining his path would call aloud and wave their petitions over their heads. Every now and again the Sultan would stop and motion to the chamberlain accompanying him, who would accept the folded paper from the fortunate man indicated and put it in a silken bag, later to be perused and judged upon. Here too was the Place of Assembly, where, under a wide-eaved porch, the throne was placed for state occasions, such as the accession ceremonies or the formal expressions of greetings on religious holidays, or for the presentation of petitions and complaints. This portico was a formalised urban expression of the part played by the clearing outside the Sultan's tent in time of war, and provided the same opportunity for reaching the royal person, although in later days the Sultan was seldom seen by his subjects except on occasions of great state.

Between the Outer and the Inner Courts stood the Middle Gate, whose double doors enclosed a small space in which those condemned to death were strangled or stabbed. A secret passage ran from it to the Divan, so that orders for summary execution could be quickly put into effect, and four mute executioners were stationed in apertures over the gate to carry out sentence as the condemned man passed through after judgment.

Other courtyards held mosques, schools, hospitals, libraries, barrack-rooms, baths and fountains, hunting- and sports-grounds and kitchens and gardens, in fact all that was necessary to maintain the pomp of a monarch known as the 'King of the Age'. The public and private apartments themselves, in the tradition of Ottoman domestic architecture, were plain and dignified on the exterior, the richness of ornament being reserved for the inside. The light, airy, summer pavilions into which the court moved in warmer weather were raised and open to catch the breezes and to provide beautiful views over the sea and shores of the Bosphorus. The interiors of the royal rooms were masterpieces of all the decorative arts that such a patron could command, but side by side with this dignity and luxury were the bustle of workshops and stables,

13 Sultan Selim II (1566–74) at a ceremony, seated on the gold and emerald throne before the Gate of Felicity in the second courtyard

14 *A palace apartment*

cookhouse and fuel-store and armoury, in fact all the myriad activities that made the Serai a city within a city. Small wonder that the Palace kitchens employed a thousand cooks and scullions who cooked for between 5,000 and 10,000 people a day, who consumed in one year 30,000 hens and 22,500 sheep, and jams, pickles, sweetmeats and sherbets in quantities which contemporary records described as simply beyond possibility of measure.

The most private precinct, rigorously separated from all other areas of the Palace, was the harem, in which all the dependent women of the household were secluded. The only passage of entry was through two consecutive pairs of doors, one of iron and one of brass. The Chief Eunuch received the keys each night from the watchman, to whom he returned them when they came on duty in the morning. Besides the Sultan and the eunuchs, the only men allowed to penetrate the harem, and then only under conditions of strictest supervision, were a few rare visiting relatives 'in the prohibited degrees', such as a father or a brother. It was a little enclosed world, fiercely guarded by detachments of Baltajis, or Wood-cutters, one of those Companies whose work covered a far wider range of activities than their titles suggest. One division served under the Chief Eunuch, and another, with its own commander, was famous for its zeal and for its long-tasselled headdresses worn like blinkers. Their barracks, completely self-contained, with dormitories, common-rooms, lockers for arms and personal effects, mosque and bath-house, lay a short distance from the harem walls. Within those walls, entered by the Gate of Felicity, the Sultan was the almost god-like master before whom none, unbidden, might speak or raise her eyes. The most important women in it were the Queen Mother and the four chief concubines—since few of the Sultans took formal wives—and these all had separate apartments and servants and rarely saw each other. Then came four categories of slaves: those who waited on the Sultan himself, those who waited on the chief ladies, those newly arrived who were still being trained for the two higher categories, and simple servants engaged on the humbler tasks. In addition there were senior women responsible for discipline and finance, and a corps of eunuch guards who formed their link with the world outside. Most of the girls were foreign slaves who were bought at the age of ten or eleven for service in the Palace, or else they came already trained as valuable gifts from rich officers and governors. Many of them eventually received their freedom and then became eligible for marriage and were, indeed, eagerly sought after since apart from their courtly graces and the charm and beauty for which they were originally chosen, they were prized for their connection with the court itself and the possibilities for influential contacts which they thus provided.

The eunuch slaves were either bought or else came as gifts presented to the Sultan by the governors of Egypt and other provinces, and were castrated by Egyptian Christians—since Muslim law forbade the practice—on the annual caravan journeys from Darfur and Sennar in the Sudan. They were trained and educated in much the same way as the Palace pages, and lived outside the harem until they were admitted into its service. There they progressed through four categories; the senior ranks acquired great power and prestige and the Chief Eunuch came eventually to be one of the highest ranking officers of the empire. The private apartments in the main part of the Palace were also to some degree staffed by eunuchs who, with the pages in training for higher office, served in such capacities as coffee-makers, pipe-lighters, turban-folders, barbers and musicians. These were members of the Inside Service, which included all the domestic staff and attendants of the residential quarters.

The Outside Service of the Palace was not exclusively concerned with Palace affairs, for these were the officials who had direct dealings with army and administrative officers, and it was through this service that the slaves rose to increasing eminence. Such traditional titles as Chief Standard Bearer, Great Master of Horse, Head Falconer and Commissioner of the Water Supply referred to posts of much dignity. The Chief Gardener, for example, was in some respects the most powerful official in the Palace, since he had 2,000 men under his control, few of whom in fact did any gardening. His were the watchmen, the guards at the gates and in the grounds, his the responsibility for policing the small ports round the Golden Horn and the Bosphorus, his a corps of the Sultan's bodyguard, the porters, grooms and bargemen; he supervised the supply to the imperial kitchen of animals and fowl for the table, the removal of refuse from the Palace precincts, and the disciplinary control of the story-tellers, tumblers and other entertainers who enlivened Palace existence. It was under his direction, moreover, that delinquent officials were interrogated and executed.

Besides the Baltajis of the harem there were four corps of guards responsible for the safety of the Palace: the archers, recruited from the Janissaries; the Sultan's magnificent personal bodyguard; the corps which served as messengers, guards and attendants; and the high-ranking Noble Guard.

The city outside the Palace consisted of a number of quarters, or mahalles, usually grouped about a mosque or, in the case of predominantly non-Muslim quarters, a church or synagogue, and each including houses, shops a bath and market. Some mahalles had a name derived from a distinguishing feature, thus Kaghithane was named after the Paper Mill which used the waters of a spring renowned for cleansing without need of soap, and the merchants who had brought bales of valuable shawls along the dusty roads from India used to dip them in the stream to wash them and make the colours fast. Tophane took its name from the Gun Foundry, where was situated the cannon which was fired to announce the rising and setting of the sun every day, and also the birth of a royal child or the death of an important traitor, the movement of the Sultan in and out of the city, the opening and closing of Ramadan and the other holy days, news of military successes, and the arrival of the grisly tribute of ears and noses to be piled at the gate of the Serai in time of war. Other quarters were named for the day of the week on which their major street market was held, like Salipazari, Tuesday Market, or else they commemorated the Anatolian or Balkan village from which the inhabitants had been brought during the resettlement, such as Yenimahalle, whose inhabitants had come from Yenishehir. Most of these mahalles had distinctive characteristics and reputations. For example, the fearsome tanners of Istanbul, who belonged to one of the oldest and most powerful trade guilds, settled after the conquest at Yedi Kule, the Seven Towers, and took over the quarantine station there in which travellers along the plague routes used to be confined for seven days before they were allowed into Istanbul. The tanners turned it into shops for themselves and for butchers—an allied trade—and it became a populous, low-class, noisome suburb of tough bachelors, for few respectable women would put up with the stench. Thieves and murderers escaping from the law were seldom pursued into the tanners' quarter, and indeed it became hardly necessary, for the tanners themselves took the criminals in hand and set them to collecting dog-dung, which was a vital component of the tanning process. As all tanners had to do this as part of their apprenticeship the task, although unpleasant, was not unreasonable, and in due course a number of these criminals rose in the craft and became master-tanners in this rough, unruly community which nevertheless could be depended on to muster 5,000 stout-hearted soldiers in time of war, and had the reputation in peace-time of being almost the only men loyal to the Sultan whom the troublesome Janissaries feared to meet in a fight.

On the other hand, the wealthy quarter of Eyub, at the top of the Golden Horn, was famous for its beauty and calm. It was the holiest Muslim place in Europe, for it was the burial-place of one of the Companions of the Prophet Muhammad, Eyyub al-Ansari, who fell in battle there against the infidel, and the district bore his name. Around his beautiful domed tomb, a place of pilgrimage, had grown up a complex of mosque and medrese, bath and almshouse, khan and bazaar, all in the dignified and satisfying architecture of the Ottoman tradition. Storks wandered about freely and nested on the domes, and, scattered down the hillside among the cypresses, were the peaceful tombs of those who had chosen to be buried, when their time came, near the tomb of the saintly warrior. In the quarter of Tersane were kept the imperial barges and their water-men, and guards lodged round about: in Kasimpasha were the imperial Arsenal and the prisons, a grim neighbourhood of harsh lives; in the gipsy quarter of Balatmahalle lived the descendants of those gipsies who had been brought from Balat, and who continued in their traditional crafts of basket-making and fortune-telling and the handling of horses, while in Kaghithane the Sultan's horses were put out to grass in the rich meadows, and the famous stream was a favourite place for picnics. Across the Bosphorus on the Asian side lay Uskudar, through which passed all the travellers from Anatolia, Arabia, Persia and India before they crossed into the heart of the city, and this district was famous for its hospices, of which it had eleven. In the one founded by Mihrimah, the daughter of Suleyman the Magnificent, a traveller might rest and arrange his affairs, staying up to three days during which time he received free lodgings, a bowl of food twice a day, a candle at night and forage for his horse or mule. Lepers were separated from other travellers at Uskudar and lodged together in a hospice outside town.

The little earth side-streets climbing up and down the slopes on which the city was built, muddy in winter and dusty in summer, with piles of rubbish and puddles of slops, led eventually to the main paved roads, cleaned and maintained by municipal workmen, in which the important buildings were situated. Individual streets were not named, but were known by the most conspicuous object in the vicinity, or by a reference to some past incident well known locally, and any stranger had to ask for identifying directions when finding his way about in an unfamiliar quarter.

The most conspicuous and important buildings in each district were the mosque and the complex of buildings that usually sprang up around it, and their provision, construction and maintenance were financed by a method peculiarly Muslim, and applicable throughout the Muslim world. Since the giving of alms was one of the pillars of Islam, all buildings and purposes which could be said to come under this heading were provided for from the revenues of private charitable bequests, called waqf. These bequests had to consist of an outright permanent gift, made either during a man's lifetime or after his death, of land or shops or some kind of immovable property which could be depended upon to bring in some permanent revenue. Money or jewels were unacceptable as being inconsistent with the immovable perpetual nature of a waqf bequest. Once the gift was made it was irrevocable and no further transfer of ownership of the property was possible, although occasionally if a large sum of money were urgently needed for the repair or improvement of the building endowed, it was possible, with the permission of the cadi, to let the waqf land out on permanent lease in exchange for the necessary sum paid as rent in advance. If the lessee died without heirs the property reverted to the waqf.

The revenues of the bequest were used for some specific purpose designated by the donor. For example, a merchant might want to give his quarter a new drinking fountain: he would assign to the waqf office a rich vineyard that he owned in the country, and with the revenues from it the fountain would be built and the façade of marble cleaned perhaps once a year, and repairs and maintenance carried out whenever necessary. He could, if he liked, appoint a trustee from his family, or some other nominee, to see that this was done according to the terms of his bequest, or he could leave it to the office to appoint an administrator. As may be imagined, the endowment made by a Sultan to build and support in perpetuity one of the great imperial mosques required a bequest of almost unimaginable wealth. Hurrem Sultan, the wife of Suleyman the Magnificent, for the provision of a public soup-kitchen, endowed it with the lake and all the lands around Tiberias, including the fisheries and the hot medicinal springs with their famous baths.

The money was administered by a completely autonomous office, independent of the Treasury and headed in an honorary capacity by the Chief Eunuch. This office appointed to each waqf an administrator—a member of the family, if this was designated by the donor—who was responsible for the collection of revenues, and a supervisor, usually a government servant or religious dignitary, who saw to it that the terms of the bequest were properly fulfilled. Often, as for example in the case of the endowment of a hospital, many people were needed for adequate implementation of the bequest, and the office appointed as many as were necessary, from the Chief Surgeon down to the man with a mop and bucket who washed the graffiti off the wall, and the pay of each employee was stipulated, down to the last lamp-trimmer and lavatory attendant. Sometimes, however, the appointments were a mere sinecure, and if the endowment had been generous the administrators themselves became extremely wealthy.

The range of purposes for which waqf money was applied was almost endless, for beside the more obvious provision for mosques and medreses, libraries and schools, hammams and hospitals, hospices and soup-kitchens and laundries, bridges and fountains, there were also dowries for orphan girls, repayment of debt on behalf of debtors in prison, burial of the indigent, clothes for the aged, rice for birds and picnics for school-children in the spring, as well as aid to soldiers and their families, and the construction and maintenance of forts and ships used in the defence of the Domain of Islam. If the object of a bequest ceased to exist, through fire or earthquake or the need to rebuild in the quarter, or for any other good reason, the waqf office applied the revenues to some other charitable purpose. Infidels, too, could make a bequest, as long as its purpose did not come into conflict with Islam; thus, they could endow an orphanage but not a church. Although a waqf had to have a charitable object, it was also possible to stretch the terms to cover the formation of a family trust in which a man's descendants enjoyed the balance of the revenues after the charitable object had benefited; this was in effect an instrument for the avoidance of taxation, offset by a public-spirited gift.

It was a natural consequence of the waqf system that the size and magnificence of the mosques, which were innumerable about the city, depended on the size and magnificence of the bequest that endowed them. The little local mesjid of the quarter was usually a simple structure, with rush mats on the floor and little decoration, and the imam would perhaps also fulfil the functions of the muezzin. The thirteen large imperial jamis, however, were the architectural marvels of the Ottoman world, with the mosque of the great architect Sinan, built by the order of Suleyman the Magnificent, the finest in the city. Monumental structures of stone, the great mosques were usually too closely surrounded by the complex of public buildings and the huddle of little houses that sprang up around them for their full majesty to be apparent to the man in the street. Only the domes crowned with golden emblems and soaring minarets against the sky hinted at the skill and complexity of the design. Once inside the court-yard, however, the calm and grandeur began to establish itself, although this too was often thronged with people, and sometimes even encamped by the army. There were little stalls where rosaries and other religious objects were sold, and booths where small dealers exposed their wares; in a corner sat the public letter-writer on a low stool, with his bright brass ink-stand and pen holder, in demand not only by the illiterate but also for his knowledge of the formulae for drawing up contracts and drafting of petitions (in fact, 'petition-writer' was the title by which he was known); by the wall perhaps a beggar waited, offering for sale a token lemon or a candle or a few nails, always waved away by the alms-giver. There were very few cases of desperate want since there were

15 Public letter-writer

many charitable organisations to
deal with real hardship, and the
Turkish tradition of hospitality as
well as the public soup-kitchens
saw to it that no-one starved; there
was, besides, always a little secure
work to be found, but so varied a

*16 Brass pen-case with ink-holder,
worn tucked in the belt*

society could always accommodate a congenital scrounger. Before the
times of prayer there was a sedate bustle round the great stone and
marble fountain, with its wide-eaved roof and ornate wrought-iron screen.

Along the façade of the mosque ran a long deep portico, supported by
columns and arches, and sometimes bordered with pieces of alternate
light and dark stone or coloured marble, ingeniously interlocked. Inside
the portico men met and talked and sat in the shade. The recessed door
of the mosque was monumental, with elaborately carved panels in
geometric designs, and sometimes inlaid with mother-of-pearl, but it was
never opened; an entrance of more modest size was cut in one of the
panels, often being closed with a leather flap hanging from the lintel. On
either side of the doorway, or inside the mosque itself, there was sometimes a stone column, six to eight feet high, which was supposed to
revolve freely in its socket when turned; if it did not this was a sign that
some slight earth tremor had displaced it from true, and the structure
was then carefully examined for weaknesses and cracks.

The interior of the mosque, as of all Ottoman buildings, was far richer
and more decorated than the exterior. The major impression, however,
was of vast reposeful space, with a great arching dome floating almost
unsupported. Soon, however, the wonderful balance of columns and
pillars and flanking rows of smaller domes resting lightly on shafts of
stone, of half-domes and arches and recesses, brought the eye to details.
The walls were decorated with tiles of glowing colours, of unmatchable
blues and greens, and a particular deep red so rich that it lay thick in
relief on the ceramic. The tiles were sometimes put together to make
whole murals of calligraphy or panels of flowers, particularly the
favourite tulips and carnations and sprays of fruit blossom. The upper
parts of the walls were pierced with windows with pointed arches,
which were usually filled according to a peculiarly Turkish design. Tiny
pieces of coloured glass were deep-set in a tracery of plaster so inclined
that the colours could only be seen from a position at a particular distance
from the window. From too close, or too far, the appearance was simply
of a curlicued stone panel. A lower tier of large clear windows, with
carved wooden shutters, was set almost at ground level, and in their
deep embrasures the theological students sat cross-legged in front of their
Koran-stands, intoning the words they were learning by heart.

Suspended from the centre of the dome, high up, was a long chain

17 Plaster window with flowers and calligraphy

from which depended an enormous iron hoop, almost as large as the dome's circumference, and from this were hung the oil lamps that illuminated the mosque at night, and sometimes also ostrich eggs brought back from the pilgrimage, or small bundles of dry stalks, the first or last cut of a harvest. The lamps hung at a height of perhaps eight feet from the ground, and effectively formed a kind of ceiling, for nothing passed through the magnificent empty vaults above except an occasional pigeon that had wandered in. The floors were covered with rugs and carpets, many of them gifts from rich members of the congregation or from groups who had combined to make a presentation to mark a holy day or memorable occasion. There was no furniture in the mosque, which served to emphasise the feeling of spaciousness. Near the mihrab which indicated the direction of Mecca was the minber, whose narrow flight of stairs led to a small pulpit under a conical roof, from which the sermon was recited. The walls concealing the sides of the stairway were of beautifully carved wood or marble, and the conical roof was richly carved or inlaid; indeed, the niche and the minber were generally objects of the finest workmanship, as befitted their role in the service. In the largest mosques there was also a raised platform supported on pillars, on which sat the muezzins, who functioned as a choir of chanters during the holy days. At the back or to one side of the main hall, behind a lattice of closely woven strips of wood, sat the women congregants, completely concealed, while in an upper gallery the ornate imperial box, also partly screened, held the Sultan and his party when he came for the Friday prayer. Except for the preachers in the imperial jamis, who were nominated by the Sheikh-ul-Islam, the ministers of each mosque were appointed and paid by the supervisors of the waqf bequest which financed it.

Non-Muslims were not allowed into mosques unless they were disguised as Muslims and had the help and connivance of a Muslim family. This might happen if perhaps a visiting diplomat who wanted to see the interior of the building gained the confidence of an intelligent man of rank, but unless he were able to perform all the prostrations he would not be allowed to remain present during the time of prayer.

Around the mosque precinct, sometimes with the geometric precision

18 Mihrab and minber in the Suleymaniye mosque

of the town planner but often in haphazard disorder, a number of buildings came to be added, the principal of these being the medreses, or centres for advanced education. Their distinctive architectural feature was the rows of small domes set in a square around an open court; the decoration within of coloured tiles, glazed bricks and marble, the colonnades and pointed entrance arches made them elegant and dignified, and when a number of them congregated round the mosque they became virtually a little university city. The students were given free board and lodging and a monthly allowance; their cell-like rooms contained cupboards and a fireplace, and these, together with the classrooms, the professors' common-room, the chapel, library and sanitary arrangements, were contained in one or two storeys around a courtyard. There was no need for cooking facilities since the students and teachers took their meals in another of the mosque adjuncts, the public kitchen. Here, every day, the poor of the district brought their containers to be filled with food and then carried them back to their families to provide the midday meal with enough left over for the evening. Those medreses which included a medical school usually had a hospital in the complex, and often also a mental hospital. The great medical school founded by Sultan Bayezid II (1481–1512) in Edirne, the second capital, had a mental hospital with individual rooms for the patients and a large hexagonal communal hall, acoustically perfect, with an open dome and a soothing fountain in the middle; at one end was a dais on which musicians sat and played to calm and distract psychopathic and melancholy patients. In most towns separate hospitals were provided for infidels, and these were also served by gifted and well-trained doctors and surgeons. The diet was always plentiful; if the hospital kitchens were found to be inadequate, food was brought in from the public kitchens.

Also to be found in the vicinity of the mosques were the libraries, in which the bound books were stored flat on shelves, and loose manuscripts tied in bundles were kept in chests. The titles of the books were written on the fore-edge, not on the spine of the binding, and the writing was always by reed pen, on glazed paper, not parchment. The binding had an additional flap which folded over the fore-edge, and sometimes the whole book was placed in an additional protective case. The floor of the library was covered with matting, on which sat cross-legged the scholars engaged on transcribing the texts; they worked only in the hours of daylight, because fear of fire prohibited any candle or flame, and smoking too was forbidden.

One of the most popular secular buildings of the mahalle was the public bath, the hammam, which was similar in design to the simpler form of mosque, having a central dome surrounded by smaller ones. Some of the largest, particularly those built over medicinal springs, had twin baths for men and women; others were built exclusively for one or the other, but the commonest were available to women only on certain days of the week, when a cloth was hung over the door as a warning to the men to keep away. Inside was a disrobing room; the larger and richer ones had private retiring rooms and also sometimes marble floors and a decorative fountain, and in any case there was always a coffee-maker crouched over a brazier bristling with the handles of copper coffee pots. Beyond, in the larger baths, was the warm room, in which there were benches for resting and massage, but all had the hot room, the central domed hall with recesses round the wall and small marble basins into which flowed the hot and cold water, to be scooped from the basin with a little brass bowl and thrown over the bather. The corner recesses were partly closed with hanging leather door-flaps for privacy. In the ceiling domes were saucer-sized apertures to let the steam escape; unless, as in Bursa, the baths were supplied by natural hot springs, the water was raised from an underground cistern by a wheel turned by an ox, and heated by the hypocaust technique used by the Romans, with a furnace beside the tanks of water, and tiled flues in the walls. When, once a month, in the great hammam built by Selim II (1566–74), twenty Palace pages with ten assistants shaved all the aghas—the heads of departments—in the Palace Service, the fires were stoked by the labours of galley slaves supplied for the occasion by the Admiralty. Some of these larger baths were extremely fine buildings, with stables, cook-shops and coffee-houses, and booths selling fruit drinks and slippers and bath-towels. All baths, being waqf endowments, were free, and though it was customary to tip the attendant there was no obligation to do so. Since, however, the baths were a great social centre, regularly visited by the people of the quarter, it would have been unwise to withhold the usual small coin and thus imperil good relations with the staff.

Certain mahalles were principally business quarters, and these were dominated by the khans and covered markets, centres of trade and commerce. The khans served the several purposes of hotel and whole-salers' offices and warehouse. They provided lodging for the night for travelling merchants, either in dormitories or in private rooms. The larger ones, usually of two or three storeys, brick or stone-built and with sloping lead-covered roofs, stood in a double lane on either side of a main street, making it a major centre for business transactions. Inside each massive gateway were rooms for the janitor and the innkeeper; around the courtyard into which it led were vaulted storerooms for baggage and animal fodder, stables and a smithy, a coffee-shop; the sleeping quarters, wash-houses and lavatories were usually on the upper storey. In some, the storerooms full of traders' goods were used as shops; in others the khan rooms served as a kind of factory, in which the raw materials which had been brought were worked into saleable goods, particularly where the strength of the building gave protective storage

19 Courtyard of a khan

at night to such valuable commodities as silver and furs. Many of these khans were built so that their revenues could support the upkeep of a mosque, for in addition to the price of their board and lodging the merchants paid for all the facilities it provided, as well as a small tax on the arrival and departure of their goods.

The markets proper were of three kinds: the bedesten, the charshi and the bazaar. The bedesten and the charshi were covered markets, single-storey buildings with a ceiling of small domes resting on pillars; they were always built beside a mosque and, like the khans, were intended to provide a permanent source of revenue for the waqf they endowed. The bedestens were originally built to store and sell silks and precious fabrics, then they began to accommodate gold and jewels and precious stones, and since there were no banks many wealthy people kept their treasures in strong-boxes and left them in the care of the bedesten shop-keepers and guards, for which service they paid a small rent to the waqf. Sur-rounding the bedestens were the charshis, covered streets of shops and booths in which the widest possible variety of manufactured goods was offered for sale. The architecture was simple and strong: they were built of stone or brick with small windows in the roof or walls to give light, for no naked flame was allowed, and they were cool in summer and warm in winter. Each aisle was devoted to the sale of one particular kind of

20 A street of armourers in a charshi

goods. In the kerchief market, for example, all kinds of embroidered articles were offered for sale: tobacco-pouches, girdles, caftans, covers for the quilts of beds and tandurs, napkins and towels exquisitely stitched. They also sold there the woven cloths from Damascus, Aleppo and Bursa which were used as wraps by bathers in the hammam, or as aprons by grocers, barbers and coffee-house keepers. There were lanes of carpet-sellers, of coppersmiths, of gold-beaters hammering the plates of metal into paper-thin leaves to be used in bookbinding and for precious inlays, and wire-workers who made untarnishable gold and silver trimmings for scabbards, saddles and ceremonial dress, sitting on the ground to draw the thread round the big toe, lanes of saddlers, druggists, cobblers ... the list was endless. The shops themselves were small, some no more than three or four feet wide, and raised from the ground. The shop booths were unornamented, and the name of the owner was nowhere to be seen on them, nor was any attempt made to display the goods to advantage or to entice the passer-by to purchase, since the wares in the charshi were of the kind that people bought when they needed them, and not on impulse. The transactions, therefore, were carried out with some dignity, and less bargaining than might be met with in the open street markets. On a wooden or stone bench that ran along the width of his shop-front sat the proprietor, and the customer would join him there and prepare for a leisurely discussion of the goods to be bought.

Business started very early in the morning, soon after the dawn prayer, and at around eleven o'clock the tradesmen would have a light meal which they had either brought from home or sent out for from a neighbouring cook-shop. All bedestens and some charshis closed at noon, others remained open until the afternoon prayer. The signal to close was always given by the gate-keeper, who struck the iron doors noisily with his keys to warn the faithful of the time of prayer and to expel the dealers, purchasers and idlers who thronged the alleyways. The shopkeeper would then draw down the door, which was hinged at the top, to cover the shop; he would throw a coarse cloth or piece of old carpet over any goods which remained in front of the door and leave, for no shopkeeper ever slept in the market. The gates were then securely locked, and the streets and aisles patrolled regularly by the market guards throughout the night.

In addition to the streets of shops, the larger markets had within their walls mosques and fountains, as well as tanks of water and fire-pumps—for the fear of fire was ever-present. The Misr Charshisi, the spice market, which was originally built of wood, suffered many small fires before it was totally destroyed in a disastrous blaze and rebuilt in 1609 of masonry, as a light airy vaulted building, to which returned the sellers of mastic and antimony, roots, seeds and dyes, henna and sandalwood and gum. In the rooms over the gate sat the commercial court where a team of judges saw

21 *Inside the Büyük Çarshi*

to it, among their other responsibilities, that no one cornered the market in any commodity, and they laid down maximum prices for goods. The Buyuk Charshi, the Great Market of Istanbul, covered an enormous area enclosed by a wall with eighteen gates. It had sixty-seven main streets, each named according to the guild installed in it, as well as dozens of side alleys, and it accommodated between three and four thousand shops in addition to mosques, warehouses, workrooms, trade schools and many other ancillaries. Its two bedestens were repositories of tremendous wealth, and were protected by their own guards and had specially accredited couriers and porters. Outside the walls a book market, a flea-market and an open food market had added themselves; the whole made the largest concentration and variety of goods for sale to be found anywhere in the world.

The bazaars, or open street markets, dealt mainly in food, and under the awnings which they stretched across the street was enacted daily a noisy bustling scene. They were usually open every day from sunrise to sunset, although some stalls closed at the time of the afternoon prayer, and at noon on Fridays. Certain bazaars excelled in the diversity and choiceness of their goods and specialities on one particular day of the week, and it was these that gave their name to the district in which they were held.

The slave market of Istanbul, near the Burnt Column, was rigidly supervised. The men were cleanly kept and humanely treated. Of the women, only the black slaves who were to be sold for menial jobs were displayed for sale; the beautiful white slaves were vigilantly secluded. Many of these had been brought from Circassia and Georgia, in South Russia, where the harsh living conditions made the prospect of harem life in a wealthy household seem far more attractive than the peasant fate that awaited them at home. They were brought in good living conditions on clean boats to the capital, where they were lodged in khans and well cared-for while they were being prepared and trained for their new lives. The best of each new consignment were selected by the Chief of the Black Eunuchs for the Serai, and the rest were sold in the market.

The law governing slavery admitted of five categories. The first were the absolute and unconditional male and female slaves. The second were slaves who were privileged to act for themselves, either conditionally or unconditionally; if the prospect of their freedom was conditional upon any event, for example the marriage of a daughter of the house, or a safe return from a pilgrimage, or the death of the owner, then a deed to this effect was registered by the cadi, and could not be upset even if the slave were subsequently sold, hired or loaned, but it did reduce his price. A slave with unconditional privileges, on the other hand, could not be sold, hired or loaned. A third category held permits which allowed them to set up in business or work on their own account. They were allowed to buy, sell and acquire property, and were responsible for their own acts and debts, but if they died childless, or intestate, their master inherited their assets, while any children they may have had, although hereditary permit-holders, were the property of the master. A fourth category had a contract by which their freedom was dependent on the payment of a certain sum or the execution of a certain task, and in the fifth came those families whose children had been acknowledged or adopted by their owners. Slaves could be killed with impunity for any offence, and the punishment of the owner was slight even for wanton killing of a slave, and he could give, sell or marry a slave to whomsoever he wished, although he could not separate married slaves. Since a slave had fewer advantages he sometimes had considerably reduced punishment: any fines or compensation he incurred had to be paid by the owner up to his value, or a slave be given in compensation, and since a slave was property, the theft of a slave child was a crime, whereas that of a free child was not.

All the markets, covered and uncovered, were constantly patrolled by inspectors of weights and measures, and in Istanbul the Chief Inspector was the Grand Vizier himself, who made a circuit of the markets each Wednesday in the company of the Chief Cadi and the Agha of the Janissaries, and on two other days independently, to ensure the proper observance of the craft and trade regulations and to punish anyone found guilty of infringing them. The market inspectors had the right to impose summary justice on any shopkeeper or stallholder who was, for example, giving short measure, and the culprit was there and then thrown on his back by two assistants while two others raised his feet between poles, presenting the soles to be beaten by the executioners with wooden rods as thick as a man's thumb. After a severe beating the unfortunate criminal would hobble painfully for days, his whole leg swollen and his guilt for all to see.

22   A street-trader punished for selling short weight

The houses of the city-dwellers were of various kinds. Those of the Grand Vizier and other notables were palaces of varying sizes, either set in gardens in the city or along the shores of the Bosphorus. Like the Serai they consisted of separate pavilions in a courtyard surrounded by high walls, sober and un-ornamented, with solid locked doorways guarded by the gate-keepers snoozing on their stone benches. The severe walls gave little indication of wealth or status: within, however, was lived out all the richness and complexity of upper-class Ottoman life. The large konaks, or town houses of the wealthier families, were sometimes set in gardens but sometimes overlooked the street. The earliest of these were light structures of wood and dried bricks, but few of these survived a hundred years, and as they fell apart they were replaced by stronger, more solid buildings two or three storeys high, with the foundations and sometimes also the ground floor of stone. The floors projected, each beyond the one below, both to increase the area of the upper part of the house and to protect the entrance and the lower walls from sun and rain. For this reason, too, the eaves of the gently-sloping roof, covered with lead or tiles, projected five or six feet beyond the upper wall. The façades were dominated by strips of windows which were normally rectangular, with decorated stone arches over them. A particular feature of Turkish architecture was the double row of windows to a single floor, the lower ones always close-shuttered against curious eyes and covered with bronze

23   *Town house of a wealthy Pasha*

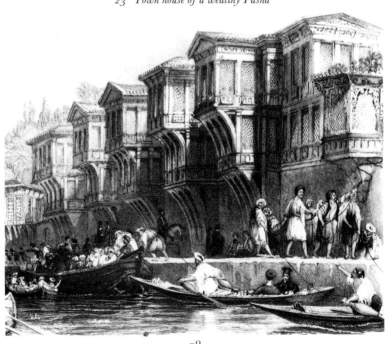

or iron gratings, the upper ones arched and filled with coloured glass panels in oval or circular plaster partitions. The windows of the upper storeys, and especially those of the women's quarters, were also covered with woven wooden shutters; curtains were never used. Some of the larger konaks contained between thirty and forty rooms, with separate hammams and stables in the gardens, and many of the families who lived in them also had gaily painted yalis, or summer pavilions on the water-side, into which they moved their entire establishment during the warmer months.

The artisans, shopkeepers, workers and lower ranks of the civil service lived in small plain dwellings; the name for this simple sort of house was ev. It was a single-storey structure, seldom more than nine feet high, usually of wood, with the roof-beams filled in with earth. Because of the terrible fires that had ravaged the city, it was ordered in 1626 that they should be built with a minimum of wood, but since this was the cheapest and easiest worked building material to hand this order was ignored. The houses lined the higgledy-piggledy little side streets of the town, and as their inside facilities were of the simplest, rubbish and slops were thrown into the road outside. To keep the thresholds clean some house-holders built a small slightly raised platform outside—a sort of large door-step—and these were a great cause of complaint by blind men who stumbled along the walls, as well as of bad feeling between families when one built higher than the others.

There was, however, one feature which was common to all dwelling-places, from palace to hovel, and that was the uncompromising separation of the women's quarters from the rest of the house. In large establishments the women might be segregated in entirely distinct buildings; in a small hut the division might consist of a thick felt cloth strung across to shut off the back part of the room; the principle was the same. The conven-tions of Muslim family life required the seclusion of the women-folk, and no home was so tiny and no family, no matter how slack in religious observance, so indifferent to this convention as to defy it.

The greatest importance was attached to the provision and distribu-tion of water, originally because the performance of ritual ablutions was integral to the practice of Islam, but also because of the part it played in the social life of the city as well as its art and architecture. Water was always deemed to be a precious gift of God, for the benefit of all nature, and it was hoarded and harvested. Cups were cut in grave-stones to catch the rain for the birds, vessels were put out even for the despised dogs in the street, and wherever a spring rose or a stream ran the Turks built a fountain, usually fronted with a slab of marble carved with an inscription from the Koran. After the conquest of Istanbul the Turks installed a new water-system, incorporating and adding greatly to that left by the Byzantines. Water from the Belgrade Forest, outside the city,

24   Aqueduct outside Istanbul

was collected by dams, stored in reservoirs, and conducted through cylindrical tiled pipes over aqueducts that crossed the ravines and valleys, through arched stone tunnels under level ground, to the gate of the city, Eghri Kapi. Thence it was filtered and passed through a succession of water towers to be distributed throughout the city. The enormous underground cisterns of Istanbul held the main supplies. Binbirdirek — the cistern of the 1,001 columns — occupied 20,000 square feet and could hold almost a million and a quarter cubic feet of water, enough to keep the entire city supplied for fifteen days. It fed the mosque fountains, the drinking fountains, the baths, the irrigation channels for orchards and gardens, and, of course, the houses, shops and factories throughout the town. The wealthier houses and more important buildings had water piped to within their gates; poorer or less accessible buildings had a cistern—sometimes a stone tank, sometimes little more than a large earthenware jar—sunk in their entrance halls. These cisterns could be reached from outside as well as within, and each day the water-carriers delivered skinfuls of water, brought on donkeys from the nearest water-store. These were huge tanks, sometimes free-standing, square, with wide sheltering eaves, marble walls and decorative railings and carved with suitable inscriptions; they were sometimes concealed behind a wall with a simple façade, set with spigots. Water was always served free to all comers; the small fee paid to the water-carriers was for the service they supplied in bringing it. The sakas who carried the thick churn-shaped skins on their backs, and delivered to the poorer houses which had perhaps only an earthenware jug in which to store it, were allocated fountains distinct from those used by the donkey- and mule-owning

water-carriers, and there was frequently conflict about poaching on each other's rights. Finally, after a formal complaint to the Sultan in 1574 by the latter group, claiming that they had '. . . served the city since the conquest and lost many horses and donkeys . . .' the Sultan issued a firman to the Cadi of Istanbul ordering him to make sure that the foot

water-carriers did not encroach any further, although the horse carriers were not to stake claims to any more fountains either. Of course, many of the poorest took their containers to the water and fetched it home themselves.

The city water department had a corps of engineers who looked after the dams and reservoirs, supervising and repairing them and making sure that no one piped off water illegally or abused the facilities which the town provided, by, for example, irrigating orchards and gardens outside the prescribed hours during periods of comparative shortage. But their pride was to keep it flowing

25 Water tank and fountain

freely, and not solely for practical use, for the Turkish ideal of pleasure and repose was to sit beside moving, running, falling water.

The large public buildings varied little in general architectural design; the main differences were rather of proportion, materials and ornamentation, and so even the most utilitarian constructions were sober, harmonious and pleasing. Among these were the state factories, many of which worked for the army and the navy. Besides the arsenals, the greatest of which were at Kasimpasha and Tophane, there were arms factories and powder factories, and others producing cloth for uniforms, bread, biscuit, boza—a beer-like drink made of barley and millet which the army drank in enormous quantities—candles and boots and all the other commodities which the military consumed at such speed. There were also factories producing goods for the Serai and the other imperial palaces, working with wood, lead, bronze and ceramics on all that was needed for the maintenance and repair of these luxurious establishments. Other factories made all the clothes for the Palace, from the uniform of the humblest servant to the rich caftans of fur-lined silk which the Sultan presented as his choicest gifts. The senior administrators of all these

26 Mausoleum at Bursa

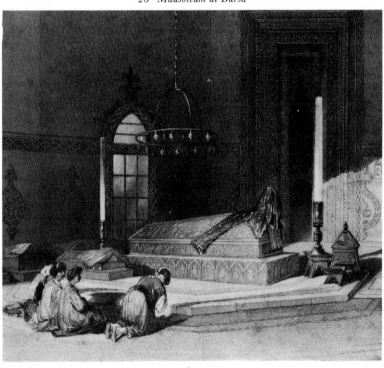

factories were civil servants; there were many non-Muslims among the artisans, and in the Imperial Mint, for example, it was usual to employ Jews.

Here and there about the city were the domed mausolea which held the tombs of the great. Of plain stone, neat and sober, their lattice-windows protected with iron grilles, they held a simple wooden catafalque with a steeply roofed lid, which was covered with shawls or sometimes a strip of the covering of the Kaaba, or of the Prophet's tomb at Medina. At its head was placed the turban of the deceased or, if it was the tomb of a woman, her head-shawl. The walls of the interior, which sometimes had a separate place of prayer, were tiled or painted with religious inscriptions; each morning the guardians repeated the whole of the Koran and a prayer for the soul of the departed. They were much visited by the faithful. Near mosques or in isolated corners of the town were smaller private mausolea which held the tombs, sometimes of a man or woman, sometimes of whole families; behind railings in odd corners of the city, too, might be a little plot with one or two graves, perhaps the shrine of a saint, at which the devout kept candles burning.

Other buildings came and went, for the city was never static. 'A Sultan never dies so long as he is building', they said, and a feature of city life was the construction work that was always in progress somewhere or other, for, both as an act of piety and a gesture of magnificence, the wealthy followed his example and gave whatever useful and beautiful monument they could afford. On the other hand the ghastly fires that constantly swept through the city left few of the older structures standing. On either side of the harbour, looking out over Istanbul, were tall towers permanently manned by watchmen who, on the first sign of smoke, beat on the enormous drum which was kept in a room at the top. The deep sound could be heard all over the city, and was particularly impressive at night, booming in the silence. The city watchmen took up the warning and told runners of the direction of the fire, and the Janissaries were dispatched to put it out. House-owners were obliged to keep their premises constantly supplied with ladders and a tank of water, and were warned not to panic and run away, leaving the whole quarter at the mercy of the conflagration.

The responsibility for policing the city was divided among a number of authorities. The Agha of the Janissaries was not only a military general but also the police officer in charge of the maintenance of order and protection of property in all of Istanbul, except for the Sultan's palace and the quarter adjacent to it. Since there was no independent police force such duties devolved on the Janissaries and other standing troops; when they were on campaign their place was taken by trainees. The area was divided into districts, to which Janissary companies were assigned for a year at a time; from their barracks patrols were sent out in per-

27 Shipping on the Bosphorus at Istanbul

manent rotation to all markets, streets and alleys. They supplied two corps of detectives for the prevention and punishment of crime and to preserve order and decorum; they often employed women detectives, and were particularly successful at recovering stolen property, possibly through some connection with the guild of thieves. They also provided a small group of spies who wandered about the city in disguise and were especially concerned with the prevention of gambling and of the neglect of religious duties, particularly by artisans whom they beat and forced to the mosque if they caught them ignoring the call to prayer; they also saw to it that children made no noise in the mosque during Ramadan. The Bostanjis' responsibility was to maintain order along the shores of the Bosphorus, the Marmara and the Golden Horn, and their chief had a list of all the houses, shops and cafés along the waterfront, over which the strictest supervision was exercised. The Kapudan Pasha, or Admiral-in-Chief, who held his own Divan, like a provincial governor, at the Admiralty, was responsible for the districts of Galata and Kasimpasha, and for the prisons to which the galley slaves were confined while they were on shore.

Never far from sight of the sea, the inhabitant of Istanbul had before him the spectacle of the greatest variety of shipping, and for many people as well as for goods water was the main means of conveyance. At anchor in the huge harbour of the Golden Horn, with spotless white

sails, fresh paint and ropes, and bright brasses, the ships of the Fleet rode majestically, a great lion carved and painted on each bow; alongside floated the pirate galleys from North Africa, slightly smaller and darker, and very business-like; then the high unwieldy merchantmen of the Black Sea, built like the ship the Argonauts had sailed through those same waters, with a single mast and mainsail; they tottered over the water and when overtaken by the northeast winds, at the end of the year, they were often driven onto sandbanks or dashed to pieces against rocks before they could gain the safety of Istanbul harbour. To prevent this manifestation of the Evil Eye they wore a wreath of blue beads hung on the prow, and took all other superstitious precautions. Dancing on the waves were also the fast light caiques, long, frail and elegant, made of thin curved polished planks of beechwood, and rowed by long free paddles bound to the gunwale with a thong of leather looped round a pin. These were used as ferry-boats, to carry a few passengers at a time from shore to shore, and all day they skimmed to and fro over the surface of the water. They were licensed to ply for hire from the wooden quays along the waterfront, each of which was supervised by a Hajji, green-turbaned to show he had made the pilgrimage to Mecca, whose silver-headed baton and badge of office were his mark of authority on that particular flight of stairs down to the water. At busy times there was much confusion and shouting of directions on the quayside, for the caiques were easily upset and had to be manoeuvred in backwards and boarded very carefully. During slacker times the caique-owners waited for customers in the coffee-houses near their 'stairs'. On the larger caiques, which acted as buses, and in which the men and women were segregated, the passengers sat on carpets and cushions at the bottom, and the rowers sat on sheepskins along the sides. Fares were fixed according to the number of oars in the caique hired, so, for example, a single-way trip up the Golden Horn in a six-oared boat cost five akches, in a four-oared boat four akches and in a two-oared boat three akches; if several passengers going in the same direction decided to share a boat each paid

28 Coffee-house on the waterside, with the caique-owners waiting

half an akche even if he got off at an intermediate stop. Any boatman
ignoring these prices was forbidden to operate, although when the sea
was rough it was allowable to charge half as much again for certain trips;
the price of longer journeys around the coast or up rivers was arranged
with the boat-owners according to a locally accepted rate. Overloading
was never allowed, nor were men and women not of one family carried
together in small boats.

29 Caiques plying for hire

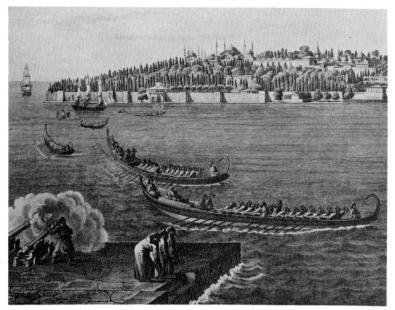

30 Naval salute

Also moving about the water might be seen the large private caiques belonging to the Sultan or some high dignitary. They had a long, up-curving prow, richly sculptured and painted, and the distinguished passenger sat under a silken canopy in the stern. The rank of the owner dictated the number of oars, which were rigidly prescribed by regula-tions, so that the guards of the watch-posts could recognise the approach of one to whom honours were due and could give the appropriate salute. The Sultan's caique was 78 feet long, painted white with gold mouldings and carvings, and had a green border along its length; its forty oarsmen were dressed in white, with blue, red-tasselled caps. In the royal proces-sion to the mosque by water six caiques took part, and the royal turban-bearer sat in the boat following the Sultan's and held up one of the three royal turbans, ornamented with herons' feathers and jewelled aigrettes, which he inclined to right and left, acknowledging on behalf of his master the prostrations, bows and cheers of the crowd. The Kapudan Pasha had an eighteen-oared ship's cutter with a particularly smart crew commanded by an officer. The Admiral sat under a canvas awning stretched on long poles from stem to stern and surmounted by crimson swallowtail banners, and the greatest etiquette was observed in the interchange of salutes with him.

The large deep clumsy barges, filled with goods or with the poorer people on their way to and from work between the city and their homes in the villages along the Bosphorus, wallowed through the water, rowed with long heavy sweeps. Here and there were also huge rafts of timber, cut in the woods of south Russia, and navigated by companies of skilled boatmen round the Black Sea and down to Istanbul, to be directed to the Arsenal for shipbuilding or to be cut up for fuel for the city.

The city woke early; after the dawn prayer most people were about their business. Their dress and turbans were of the widest variety. Shortly after the capture of Constantinople, Sultan Mehmed the Conqueror laid down the regulations by which the clothes of the civil and military hierarchy were to be distinguished, and the shapes and colours of the outer garments of all ranks were specified and adhered to with only slight variations until 1826. Thus, the upper ranks had turbans of various colours wound round tall felt caps; members of the ulema had lengths of dazzling white muslim bound round gold-embroidered skull-caps, which gave the completed turban a much flatter shape. These snowy turbans and the sombre black gowns of the religious dignitaries and medrese students, the rich caftans and head-dresses of the aghas, the naval officers and Arsenal guards with knives in their belts, the dervishes in homespun, the street scavengers in red leather smocks, with brooms and wooden shovels, the gipsies with their dancing bears, all contributed to the vivid scene. In the wealthier quarters important personages rode to their offices, sometimes accompanied by their attendants; in the poorer side-streets the artisans and labourers and humble clerks stepped over the heaps of rubbish on their way to work.

31 Sherbet-seller

Shutters were raised, colourful goods were hung outside: skeins of bright silks drying over the dyers' doorways, rows of copper pans, bundles of slippers.

Down the lanes came the cries of the street vendors, peddlers of fruit and vegetables, tinkers and water-carriers. The first calls in the morning, and the last at night were those of the milkmen and yoghurt sellers. To the cry of 'Igde!', a sweet syrup, very popular with the ladies, was carried round the town in casks on the shoulders of certain sturdy Anatolians who had brought it in from the country, and who had a particular reputation as wits and seducers. The sellers of sherbet and fruit drinks, on the other hand, did not shout but clinked together musically the glasses or metal cups in the trough round their waists. They carried the sherbet on their backs in containers with a long thin spout that arched over

88

the shoulder, and they bowed slightly to pour the liquid accurately into the glass held at waist level before them. 'Buy my apples! Peaches!' called the apple-seller, naming first the fruit he had for sale, and then the more luxurious one which he implied his wares resembled. 'Destur'—'Permission'—shouted the porters in warning of their coming, bowed under such burdens that they could not raise their eyes from the ground. And at Ramadan or Bayram, or whenever some piece of news made it necessary, the town criers with their drums circulated the quarters, stopping here and there to collect a crowd and give out their information. And in the workshops hammers fell and sparks flew and stones cracked under the pick.

But with all this activity there was no undue scramble or haste, and except for the occasional brawling of a group of drunken Janissaries it was rare to find disorder or loud quarrels in the street. The pace generally was deliberate and unhurried; haste and unseemly noise were avoided. The very street cries, by their familiarity and regularity, formed part of the pattern and permanence of the street scene. Yet this absence of pressure, together with the Turk's innate love of nature and beauty, also made possible the improvisation of circumstances of great charm. Sometimes, for instance, a coffee-seller would stop at a place that caught his fancy—perhaps a tree in flower or an unexpected view, or even some small incident in the street. He would set up in business for half a day or so, and other itinerant salesmen, a sherbet-seller, the man with his stock of bubbling nargilehs, the boys with trays of sweetmeats, and the entertainer with his performing monkey would collect round him, and a little centre of pleasurable activity was set up for the enjoyment of the passer-by who would settle for a short while on the rush-bottomed stools provided by the coffee-seller, and then be on his way. Towards evening, when the coffee-man moved off, the others would also disperse, and by nightfall it was as though the little transient encampment had never been, and indeed it might never be exactly there again.

The activities of the city were governed by the length of the day: by the mid-afternoon prayer all the main markets and offices were closed, and by nightfall there was scarcely a soul to be seen on the streets. The police discouraged any sort of traffic, and anyone who had to be abroad was obliged to make his presence known by carrying a torch or candle, and only the blind were exempted from this since they might, unaware, start a blaze from their uncovered flame. Except for the executioner, whose emergence from the Palace and appearance on the street after dark signified that he was about his grisly duties, most people were safely within doors, and only the raucous cry of the night-watchman as he made his rounds, and the thud of his iron-tipped staff along the cobblestones, disturbed the silence of the night.

5

Family Life

In Ottoman Turkey there was, generally speaking, a complete absence of any hereditary aristocracy among the subjects of the Sultan. There was no class of society which could be said to be privileged by reason of birth, and there were very few powerful families; indeed, family names were practically unknown. All Muslim subjects were equal before God, and this provided conditions in which great social mobility was possible. Not only could a man of ability rise to the greatest heights in the learned professions but, except for the whim of a capricious Sultan, it was impossible to do so without merit. Similarly, so great was the respect for trade that any man who had become wealthy through skill or hard work in the field of commerce was accorded the greatest esteem, no matter how humble his origins. Even slavery was considered a kind of misfortune of chance, and there was absolutely no feeling that any man or class of men were natural slaves, or that the condition was irreversible, and in all cases of emancipation they immediately possessed full civil, legal and social rights, their previous condition counting for nothing. On the other hand, opportunities for advancement were offset by a widespread acceptance of the existing structure of society and of each individual's place in it, as well as a very general tendency for sons to follow their fathers into the same line of work. In all classes of society there existed a natural self-respect and dignity, a sense of the intrinsic worth of each man and of his right to justice. Although in battle the Turks could prove themselves ferocious and merciless, especially towards the enemies of Islam, in their private lives they were on the whole calm, mild and self-controlled, and capable of great gentleness and humanity. The teachings of Islam encouraged charity, cleanliness and sobriety, but to these virtues the temperament of the Turks added qualities of integrity and decorum not always shared by other peoples within the empire.

Beyond his vague but overriding sense of duty to his Sultan, the loyalties of an average Ottoman subject were practical and immediate: if he lived in a city he thought of himself first and foremost in relation to his guild; if he lived in the country his responsibility was as a member of his village community, and his life outside the family was governed by the duties and rights of membership of those bodies. Within the family, the master of the household had absolute authority over the two or three generations under his roof. For all unmarried daughters lived at home, and a young apprentice son would bring his bride home too; in addition a widowed mother, or unmarried aunt or sister, or some other helpless dependant might be the responsibility of a working man. Room would have to be found in his house for all of them, and he would have to provide for their needs; it was inconceivable that he should shirk his duty in this respect. Among the rich, huge family groups lived in the large rambling houses: the mother, who ruled over all the women-folk, the married sons and their families, single sons, unmarried or divorced daughters, grandchildren, concubines, servants and slaves, all under the patriarchal domination of the father. But here again the Turkish character reinforced the teaching of Islam, and the authority of the head of the household was tempered by moderation and generosity. A natural awe surrounded his position, and the household was always gayer and less constrained when he—and any other senior men in the family—were away from home, but he was usually a reasonable, and even affectionate, family man.

The difference between the conduct of wealthy households and more modest homes was mainly one of degree, not kind: in rich establishments, for example, the slaves would do the marketing, while among working-class families the husband would bring the shopping home, but in neither case did the women of the house go out to the bazaar to get the food, and they would make only small purchases from the street traders who came to the door. Rich and poor shared customs and superstitions: all had the same family occasions and seasonal festivities, the same love of nature and contempt for non-Muslims, the same standards of hospitality, the same fear of childlessness and pride in their sons. The celebration of public and private occasions differed in the pomp and display of wealth; all families did the best they could afford. Also, a peculiarly intimate relationship existed between a family and its servants. It is difficult to say whether this was a cause or result of their respectful familiarity with each other, but certainly when conversation between master and employee, and, even more commonly, mistress and maid, was so personal and free, and the servants were so much part of the family itself, the wealthy could not fail to be kept in touch with the thoughts and feelings of the poorer classes.

Life was regulated by the hours of prayer, which were timed by the call of the muezzin, and so there was no need for clocks. There were some sundials on public walls, and a few water clocks in mosques and medreses for fixing the time of prayers. That in the Imperial Mosque at Beyazit, for example, fixed the time for the whole of Istanbul. The period of activity was regulated by the hours of daylight since lighting was expensive and poor, and thus the short winter days afforded little time for social activity. The prayers at home, which were generally those of dawn, evening and night, were said on a little rug kept for the purpose, which was spread on the ground pointing in the direction of Mecca. The midday and mid-afternoon prayers would be said either at work, where at the appointed hour each man unrolled his small rug and made his prostrations, or in a nearby mosque. Usually the whole family went to the jami for the Friday noon prayer.

All washed when they rose in the morning: they wiped their teeth, passed a wet hand over face and head, and washed their hands and arms. The men dressed in trousers, shirt and dolman, and wound a wide sash around the waist into which they tucked their tobacco. A handkerchief, money, and anything else they might require was placed in the breast of the garment above the belt, and this acted as a kind of pocket. Over all they wore a caftan, which among the wealthy could be a garment of great luxury. Attached to the trousers were fine leather socks, over which they wore soft-soled leather slippers. For outdoor wear a pair of strong, heavy yellow leather shoes were put on over the slippers, or, for riding, thick loose black boots. The turban, a length of muslin or other cloth, was wound round a felt cap, in distinctive style. Poorer men wore simply trousers, a shirt and a waistband, with a soft cap or cloth tied round the head. Although beards were not obligatory all members of the ulema wore them, as well as many teachers and civil servants, and they added considerable dignity; heads were usually shaved.

A woman of the working class wore full trousers to the ankle, and a smock, and although she had slippers and overshoes for the street she was usually barefoot in the house. The dress of women of the middle and upper classes could be extremely elaborate. They too wore full trousers, and over them a fine gauze smock edged with embroidery, with a high neck and sleeves to the elbow. Over this came a tight buttoned waistcoat with long sleeves which fell back over the arms, and a close-fitting ankle-length caftan, tied with a girdle. Over this, in cold weather, they wore a loose robe of brocade lined with fur, and a tasselled cap. Over their soft leather socks they wore heelless slippers with up-curved points, richly embroidered and decorated, and even the street overshoes were ornamented.

Men wore little jewellery other than rings, but the women had as much as their men-folk could afford: rings, earrings, pendants, necklaces, bracelets, jewels in their headdresses and strings of pearls across the kerchief which was draped over their felt caps. Among poorer women, the gold coins with which they decorated their headscarves, and their gold earrings and bracelets, represented the entire capital wealth of the family.

The cycle of family events—birth, circumcision, marriage and death —was further punctuated by occasions which it was customary to mark in some way. The first day at school, admission to full membership of a guild, the return of a pilgrim relative from Mecca, all were accompanied by the traditional ceremonies that formed so large a part of family life.

As might be supposed, the birth of a baby was an occasion particularly within the province of the women. A son was always most ardently wished for, and throughout the pregnancy many superstitious practices were resorted to in an attempt to ensure that the baby was a boy, but children were so much loved that the safe delivery of a healthy infant was always a cause of rejoicing. The midwife, a woman much respected in the community, had been hired from the sixth or seventh month, and all the necessary preparations made. The swaddling bandages, fine cotton smock, blue shawl and bonnet and the amulet against the Evil Eye were collected together to the recitation of blessings, sprinkled with sesame seeds as a further precaution against the Eye, tied in a bundle and hung on the wall facing the direction of Mecca. A bag containing the Koran was hung over this bundle.

As the time of birth approached, the midwife's walnutwood birth-chair was brought to the house, a sign for the neighbouring women to offer their help and for the menfolk of the household to remove them-selves. During labour the mother sat on the horseshoe-shaped chair, gripping the arms, while the midwife recited 'Allah akbar'—'God is most great'—and the Declaration of Faith, all present joining in. When the baby was born it was washed and the umbilical cord was cut, at which time the child was given its first name. Three sesame seeds were placed on the navel and the baby was then bound, swaddled and dressed; the blue-bead amulet tied with a red ribbon was pinned to the shoulder of its dress, from which position it could protect the child from danger both from front and back. The mother was put to bed on mattresses covered with specially rich shawls and quilts, with matching side-pillows to prop her up. Over the bed hung a Koran, under it was placed an onion on a spit. hung with garlic and blue beads, and around it a broom and whatever other defences had been found efficacious against the Eye, for both mother and child were particularly vulnerable in the first days. At the bedside stood a bottle of sherbet, with red gauze tied over the top if the baby were a girl and round the neck if it were a boy. Similar bottles were sent to friends and relations as notification of the birth, and visitors began to arrive with gifts tied in embroidered handkerchiefs—for kerchiefs large and small, plain and decorated, were used for wrapping, tying and conveying

32 *Birth-chair*

all gifts—and to offer congratulations in the formula also used when a loved one returned after an absence, 'May your eyes be bright'. The head of the family then gave the child its second name: he held the baby up to face Mecca and recited the Call to Prayer and the Declaration of Faith into its right ear, and into the left certain verses from the Koran and, three times, the new name which was usually historical or the name of some semi-legendary hero.

Poorer women returned to their duties very shortly after the birth of their babies, particularly in the countryside; others stayed in bed for three to six days, receiving in state, dressed like a bride. Often this was literally true, for among the less wealthy the dress that had been prepared for a girl's marriage was her finest, and it would be put in a chest after her wedding and brought out only on occasions of rejoicing. On the seventh day there was sometimes a party, with Koranic chanting or other music, at which the baby's cradle, usually a present from the maternal grandmother, was ceremonially produced. These were sometimes richly inlaid with silver or mother-of-pearl, and not a few were heirlooms. Then the mother's special bed was removed and life began to return to normal. On the fortieth day after the birth, however, there was a further ceremony, this time at the hammam. The mother, richly dressed and accompanied by the midwife and friends, went to the bath and paraded round the fountain in the cool-room. Aloes-wood was burned in a silver censer and music played, and all present came to congratulate her. When the mother and her party had finished the ritual of the greeting and then the bath, the midwife took the baby from its basket in the corner and unswaddled it. She wrapped it in a shawl and took it into the bath for the 'forty' ceremony: a duck's egg was broken into a bowl, and after the baby had been washed with a soft soapy cloth the egg was rubbed all over its body, to accustom it to water, like a duck, and to keep it safe in that element. The midwife then let the water flow over a gold piece while she recited from the Koran and repeated a Fatiha, and the baby was washed in the water, then dried and swaddled and dressed again. This too was the occasion of small gifts, of silver bells or amulets of protective prayers in little embroidered bags, a silvered wolf's tooth, perhaps, or a bone teething-ring, or blue beads with seven holes.

Many children were given to a wet-nurse for suckling, and this established a very strong link, for the children of a wet-nurse were treated like the brothers and sisters of the nursling and were subsequently in the prohibited degrees for purposes of marriage; the nurse herself became the baby's 'milk-mother', and however humble her rank had been she was always thereafter accorded the utmost respect by the family and especially the child throughout its life.

Teething was another milestone, and the appearance of the first tooth was welcomed with rejoicing, as were the child's first unsupported steps;

as soon as it began to totter it was put into a little four-wheeled cart just high enough for its feet to touch the ground, and so it learned to walk. Children were weaned at around the age of two, girls usually before boys, and this was another occasion for a party at the hammam, at which they were smeared with mother-of-pearl oil before being ceremonially washed. When babies cried they were given comforters made of a knob of marzipan tied in a knot of cloth, but many nurses and busy mothers also gave them soothing drinks of poppy-head water and other narcotics to keep them quiet, less because the noise was troublesome than because they feared that the crying baby was unhappy.

Although all children were dearly loved, and in rich homes even spoiled and indulged, they were imbued from the earliest age with the greatest respect for older people, and in particular for members of their own families. This deference was shown to father, mother, elder brother and elder sister, and even an adult son would never sit, eat or smoke in the presence of his father without his permission. Want of respect, and disobedience to parents, were considered sins equal in gravity to idolatry, murder, false witness and desertion in the holy war, and this importance given to the inculcation of a proper attitude towards authority had a stabilising effect beyond the family, for a man's deference to his elders was readily translatable into loyalty towards an authoritative State.

At the age of five the children, and in particular boys, were taught to perform the ritual ablutions and prayers, and learned at their mother's and grandmother's knee the stories and fables of Turkish legend. At about the age of seven, and even earlier if the family could afford a private tutor, the little boys were taken from the harem, that is, away from the exclusive influence of the women of the house, although the mother never lost her authority and responsibility for certain aspects of her son's life. If the boy had a lala, or private tutor, he would begin his studies at home, and when he had outgrown all that his lala could teach him he was put into care of a hoja, a wise man, who would complete his education. But most children went to school, in a simple stone building attached to the mosque. There were usually a large number of these Koran schools in the towns, sometimes in an upper-storey room over a mosque fountain. In the villages, where there were few ancillary buildings, the mosque itself might be used as a school-room between the dawn and the mid-morning or noon prayers.

On his first day, his father took the boy to kiss the teacher's hand, and saying, 'His flesh is yours, his bone is mine', meaning, 'Chastise him if you think he needs it, but send him back to me', he left the child to begin his school life. First day at school was often an occasion of celebration: sometimes the boy was put on a little horse and, escorted by a chorus of children chanting and of men giving the responses, he would make a tour of the saints' tombs to make vows and ask for their help. The school-

95

33   A prince's school-book bag

master, appointed by the waqf supervisor of the mosque, was usually a pious man of no great intellectual attainment, but it would have been unthinkable for the children to treat him with anything less than the devoutest deference; and especially in the poorer quarters, where there was great reverence for any kind of learning, many parents sent along little presents for the teachers. Some private teachers of greater ability were occasionally to be found, either employed by a more academically-minded waqf authority or by a group of the parents themselves, but generally the standard was low.

School was one big room, with the schoolmaster's seat and desk at one end, his cane and bundle of sticks on either side of him. In a corner stood a long thin rod with which he could reach to slap the children at the back, so none were out of reach although he remained undisturbed, cross-legged on his cushion; minor offences were punished by making the children stand for some time on one leg, with their hands in the air. When a boy wanted to leave the room he would stand in front of the teacher with one foot on the other and his hand raised, and the hoja would give permission. The boy would then turn a board hanging on the wall so that it read 'Gitti'— 'Gone'. When he came back he would turn it over, so that it read 'Geldi' — 'Come', and only one boy was allowed to leave the room at a time, so that a busy or drowsy teacher could keep a simple check on absences. The class sat cross-legged on the floor, the newest boys in the front, and recited by heart whatever they were learning, for the school work consisted almost entirely of memorising, which was thought to be aided by a rhythmic rocking to and fro. First they learned the alphabet, then they began to recite the Koran, then to chant it. They learned the correct gestures, prostrations and intonations of prayer. When, one great day, a boy had reached a stage which the teacher considered satisfactory, he was sent home in the middle of the morning, and this was considered a high honour. People in the street, seeing the proud child with his school-bag at the unaccustomed time of day stopped to congratulate him, and the family made a great fuss of him. But by the time the child had learned some calligraphy and perhaps to read a little and to do a few simple sums the teacher's ability was usually exhausted, and for many children education ceased at this stage.

Children went to class every morning of the week except Friday, but there were many interruptions of the school year for holidays of various kinds: religious, guild, imperial as well as family festivals. In the spring particularly there were often school journeys by ox-cart for picnics in the country. These were paid for by the waqf endowment, which also provided poor children with new clothes and shoes for the occasion; in fact there were certain markets which sold ready-made clothes for this purpose, an unusual commodity as most garments were made for the customer, however poor, by a tailor. Another excursion which fell to the hoja and children as a kind of duty took place during the dry season, when their intervention was considered to be particularly effective against drought. The party went to the country, and after certain very old rain-making rites involving stones or horse-skulls or whatever was the custom in the locality, everyone would turn his clothes inside-out, and the schoolmaster would recite the prayers for rain. The children would let their hands hang down, open and empty, and reply 'Amin', and the community would then confidently await God's mercy.

As there was no control or supervision of the teaching it was not surprising that the standard of these Koran schools was undistinguished. There were a few better primary schools, some maintained by dervish sects for the children of their adherents and some run privately, but at least there was a form of education available to all, and although the poorest children usually finished school very young and went to work, if a boy had a particularly scholarly bent he could continue his education all the way through the medreses, at no cost to his parents. Those boys who continued school after the age of about twelve went to lessons given in the mosque by a member of the ulema, whose standard of education was a good deal higher. These classes lasted from morning prayer until the shops, markets and offices opened, when many boys went off to help their fathers or earn a little money in any unskilled way available to them. At these lessons they might study Arabic and Persian grammar, ethics, learn a little poetry by heart, and perhaps acquire some more arithmetic. Rich boys usually continued their education, and those of the middle class who did not become merchants or professionals like their fathers were eventually directed into some fitting career. Most sons of artisans and tradesmen and lesser clerks soon went into their fathers' occupations as apprentices, and the occasion of their eventual admission into the guild of their craft was a landmark in the life of many young men. Would-be clerks had to pass a rather unexacting examination, including the correct cutting and folding of envelopes, and schoolboys accustomed to keeping a silkworm cocoon in the inkwell to absorb the ink and prevent a messy spill had to demonstrate the proper maintenance of writing equipment.

Those boys, however, who were really determined to become members of the learned professions continued their higher education in the medreses, whose size and importance, as well as the quality of their teaching, were dictated by the generosity of the endowment. There were medreses attached to all the imperial mosques, and altogether there were perhaps eighty-five such teaching establishments in Istanbul alone. The length of time spent on this grade of education depended on how high the candidate wished to rise in the ulema. The subjects studied were mainly theological in scope and there was little work in the more rational disciplines, such as astronomy or mathematics or natural history. Medicine, because of its charitable connotations, was more acceptable, but the ulema were opposed to all new ideas, and this conservatism, together with their abomination of the printed word as an irreligious innovation, made the dissemination of new and useful information virtually impossible, and the slaves in the Palace School probably received better instruction in secular subjects than did the students of the great medreses.

Girls seldom received much education, but were trained at home in sewing and embroidery, or helped their mothers in the house and on the land. Very few ever learned to read or write, although they too were able to say the prayers by heart, and absorbed in addition a wealth of traditional lore of which the women were the custodians.

The greatest occasion in the life of a boy was his circumcision ceremony, a practice nowhere to be found mentioned in the Koran but an indispensable *rite de passage* for all male members of the Muslim faith. The ceremony was entirely secular, and there were no special prayers. Some babies were circumcised on their fortieth day, but most underwent the operation between the ages of five and twelve, and particularly at the age of seven or eight. Where there were in a family two or more brothers fairly close in age there was a joint ceremony at a convenient average time, and sons of poor people frequently shared in the arrangements and festivities of the rich if they had reached a suitable age. For some days before the great occasion the boys wore distinguishing blue satin hats, and sashes across their silk shirts, so that even strangers in the street recognised its imminence and greeted them with good wishes. At this time, too, every precaution was taken against the dreaded Eye, and in some of the eastern provinces the boys were even known to wear female dress and ornaments borrowed from the women of the household, and cover their faces with a handkerchief to delude the powers of misfortune that they were mere female

34 Circumcision hat, with silver thread embroidery and spangles

35 Public festivities to celebrate the circumcision of a Sultan's son

creatures and so avert their jealousy, but most young Turks thought this a
cowardly act at a time when they should be demonstrating their fitness
to pass into the world of men.

On the day, the surgeon-barber arrived and prepared the room. The
boy wore a new silk robe, with matching stiff cap decorated with
sequins. He stood on a table, feet astride; one man grasped his ankles
firmly, another pinioned his arms from behind, and the operation was
swiftly performed with a sharp razor and the wound cauterised with
wood-ash. When a number of children were to be operated upon, two
or three were brought into the room at a time, and were exhorted to
outdo each other in bravery. Clowns and tumblers who had waited in
hiding leaped into the room to distract the children, and outside the
house the drummer walked up and down, beating loudly, both as a
signal that the moment had arrived and to drown any unmanly cries.
The boys were put to bed, perhaps two or three together, between sheets
strewn with little black seeds against the Eye, their caps laid over the
affected parts to keep off the weight of the bed-clothes. All the guests
came to congratulate them on their entry into manhood and to give them
suitable presents. It was an occasion of great pride to the whole family;
the circumcision of a Sultan's son was an occasion of national rejoicing.
In all cases the house was decorated and the richest food and entertainment the father could afford was provided for the guests; the women of
the household and their female visitors watched the entertainment from
behind screens. From this time the boy was finally excluded from the
harem and became one of the men of the family; his training and future
were entirely under the jurisdiction of his father.

Eventually the father would decide that the boy had reached an age
when he ought to be married, and it was then that the role of the mother

reasserted itself, for it was her reponsibility to choose him a wife. The mother of a marriageable son was naturally in a position of great power, and if she had not already made a choice in her mind she began to enquire directly of acquaintances about a suitable match. Sometimes, through an intermediary, the mother of a boy might hear of a likely bride, and would arrive unannounced with two or three friends, perhaps at the house of a perfect stranger, and ask to see the daughter they had heard of. The party was gladly admitted, and while the lady of the house entertained them the girl was quickly dressed up for inspection. It was her duty, when she was ready, to bring in the richest coffee-set the household possessed and serve the visitors, her head modestly cast down. The inspection was long and frank and sometimes extremely nerve-racking for the young girl, who was obliged to submit to it until the senior visiting lady returned her coffee-cup, and at this signal the girl withdrew. Sometimes several girls were scrutinised before a final choice was made; occasionally inspection of the girl took place at the hammam. The young man's mother let it be known that she would be at the bath with her party on a certain day and desired the presence of the girl, who would duly appear with her mother and friends, and although the inspecting party made no secret of the reason for their coming, sometimes with audible comments either favourable or unfavourable, it was the difficult task of the girl and her group to behave as naturally and modestly as possible, and, while displaying her suitability, appear to know nothing of the purpose of the visit.

If she approved of her the boy's mother would ask for her hand in marriage on his behalf, and the girl's mother would then enquire about the boy's work and prospects, and that evening both mothers would consult their husbands and put the arrangements into their hands. If the boy's family was unknown to the girl's father he would immediately start enquiries among his friends. At this time good dreams were considered to be fortunate omens and bad dreams would often delay arrangements for a considerable time; if the father's investigations proved that the boy was an unsatisfactory suitor the girl's family would say at this point that the omens had been unpropitious and that the project would therefore have to be abandoned, and so the matter was concluded tactfully. In less wealthy homes the arrangements were correspondingly less complex. The boy's mother, perhaps with the advice of some female relation, made the choice for him and described the girl to him, and the two fathers or nearest male relatives completed the technicalities between them; the girl's family seldom made any objection unless the boy was very obviously totally unacceptable.

Mothers of girls, on the other hand, would begin to plan for their daughters' weddings as soon as they were born. After the age of twelve or so girls veiled their faces and were considered marriageable. Matchmakers began their visits, their intriguing, and their exaggerated descriptions of the wealth and charms of both sides, and mothers intensified their work on the trousseaux which they and their daughters had been working on for some years. One of the more pleasurable occupations, in fact, in households in which there was a marriageable girl was the preparation of her clothes and linen as well as of precious heirlooms, which were tied in embroidered cloths and stored against her wedding-day when they would be displayed as a demonstration of wealth and good taste.

Girls were married without either their consent or their approval, and boys were not much consulted either. Sometimes families who wished to be linked promised their children to one another in babyhood : among artisan families the father usually had a strong preference for a son-in-law in the same trade as himself. In all circumstances the compatibility of the two families was of decisive importance in the choice, and except among some peasants, or the poorest element in the town among whom conditions of the strictest propriety were not always rigidly maintained, the groom never saw his bride's face or spoke to her until the conclusion of the wedding celebrations.

Marriage was purely a civil matter, devoid of sacraments. When both sides had come to an agreement the boy and girl exchanged betrothal gifts, the marriage contract was drawn up and a copy given to each side. Any sums of money involved, such as the contribution of the groom's family to the cost of the wedding, and the amount of the girl's dowry of which part was kept back in case of divorce, were, after some haggling, agreed on to the satisfaction of both sides. If there were no impediment of kinship, such as ties of blood or marriage or milk, nor of religion, for whereas a man might marry a Christian or a Jew, a woman could only marry a Muslim, the contract was completed. It was witnessed by two Muslims and made publicly known in the quarter, at which point it became valid and binding and the date of the wedding feast to celebrate it was fixed. The most auspicious day was considered to be a Friday; the next favourite choice was Monday.

The extent of the festivities that preceded this depended on the wealth and circumstances of the two families. Some had their feast that very day, and the bride went home with the groom to live in his father's house, but for families who could afford it the celebrations lasted a week, during which the young man sent his unknown bride many traditional gifts of jewellery and toilet articles, as well as large trays of fruit and sweetmeats for her family. The girl reciprocated with a jewelled tobacco box or perhaps richly embroidered slippers, and her messenger would bring back a description of the illuminations and decorations in the groom's quarter.

On Monday the bride's family sent the groom's wedding outfit to his

36 A wedding procession

house, and in the afternoon certain of her older female servants, including her nurse, with silk sashes across their shoulders, rode on
donkeys to the houses of the bride's friends and, announced by men with
kettle-drums, invited them to accompany her to the hammam and to a
party on the following day. On Tuesday at around noon the bride and
her guests went in state to the hammam, preceded and followed by
musicians, men carrying utensils and linen, the water-carrier, the per-
fume-carrier and other attendants. The bride herself walked under a
brightly-coloured silk canopy carried by four men with poles, with an
embroidered handkerchief tied to the top of each. In hot weather a
woman attendant walked backwards in front of her waving a fan of black
ostrich feathers. Sometimes the whole bath-house was taken over by this
bridal group with its music and entertainments, and at the washing
ritual great care was given to the bride's toilette, with rare oils and perfumes, after which they all returned for a banquet in the bride's house.

The following night, the men were entertained at a noisy party in the
groom's house, with music and dancers, including gipsy girls who
performed with their faces unveiled, a spectacle that the ladies of the
household thoroughly disapproved of. They, however, had a party of
their own in the bride's house in honour of Henna Night. On this evening
the bride's hands and feet were stained with the orange paste; a gold
piece, which was thereafter treasured for luck, was smeared with henna
by the bride's mother and tied in the palm of the girl's right hand, and
both hands and feet were bound with strips of linen to keep the stain on
all night. On Thursday came the groom's presents of clothes to the bride.

When she was dressed, and her forehead, cheeks and chin stuck with sparkling sequins, the matron of honour brought her out on display, and the bride kissed her father's hand. He then tied a shawl around her waist and brought out his sword which he extended for her to jump over, saying: 'Bring forth offspring who will use this sword well, like your ancestors.' Then he recited suitable prayers, and on this solemn occasion all present wept, for this was her last day at home and the real end of her childhood.

On Friday the bride was led in procession to the groom's house, and taken to the bridal chamber where she sat in a corner which had been decorated as a bower, with silken hangings and embroideries. Around the walls were displayed all her wedding gifts and the contents of her trousseau, the richest objects hanging at eye-level and the linen and lesser articles above. Jewels and precious gifts were displayed in alcoves, and the whole room was hung with garlands of coloured silk flowers and had been arranged by the bride's friends to achieve the most beautiful effect possible. All day long, guests came to bring her presents and to inspect her clothes and trousseau, to praise and criticise. Meanwhile the groom and his friends had been taken in procession with drums and music to the mosque; on his return, with a great show of reluctance, and considerable real shyness, he was finally escorted and jostled to the door of the bridal chamber, to cries of 'The groom is coming!'. There, partly led by the matron of honour, partly pushed by his friends, he entered to meet his bride, who rose to kiss his hand, and when she removed her veil they came face to face for the first time. He gave her a 'Face-See' gift to mark the occasion, usually a jewel, and embraced her, but only stayed with her for a few moments, and then rejoined the men in their quarters, while the bride and her guests all went into the reception room of the harem and, separated as ever, the two groups celebrated the wedding feast. Whatever else the meal consisted of, rich and poor alike served a huge dish of wedding rice tinted yellow with saffron—no wedding would have been complete without it. Thereafter the bride became a member of her father-in-law's household, her chief concern to please her husband's mother by the production of a grandson.

The first wedding of a boy and girl, chosen as much for the agreeable union of two families as in the hope of happiness for the young couple, was the one celebrated with the greatest delight by all, but since a Muslim was permitted as many as four wives on the condition that he provided each with a separate and equal establishment, and since a widow or divorced woman was a great responsibility to some unfortunate male relation until he could marry her off again, many marriages were contracted with considerably less ceremony.

It was difficult for a woman to divorce her husband; unless her right to do this was included in her marriage contract or she was rich enough to buy him off, it was necessary for the cadi to adjudge her case and decide whether her claim was reasonable. Men, on the other hand, were subject to no such control and were able to divorce their wives on the merest whim. In fact, among certain classes, it was more common to marry and divorce frequently than to suffer the expense of a full quota of four wives at once, each with her separate dwelling. This made the position of many women extremely precarious, and accounted for the docility with which they accepted their subordinate position. A man might divorce his wife simply by reciting the formula: 'I divorce you'; he could do this twice and take her back each time without ceremony, but if he repeated the formula a third time and wished to remarry her, she had to be married and divorced by another man before this was possible. Thus, any man who divorced his wife in a temper for the third time, and repented of it, would hire some poor old man to marry her for the space of one night, as was required, and divorce her next day. If, however, the husband meant the divorce seriously and permanently, his wife could not remarry until three months had passed, and if meanwhile she proved to be pregnant she had to wait until the child was delivered, and her husband was responsible for her maintenance throughout this time.

Legal separation without divorce was also possible. A husband could chastise his wife in moderation, and restrict her to the house except for an occasional visit to her parents, and a wife had to be obedient to her husband provided his orders were not dangerously unreasonable, but if the cadi considered that her complaints were justified he would allow her to return to her parents. She could also be granted a separation if her husband was unable to maintain her, but in this case her father or the male relation to whom she would return usually preferred to contribute to her upkeep while she remained under her husband's roof, hoping to be repaid by him when his situation improved.

If a husband wished for a separation from a tiresome or shrewish wife, he would take her, or, if she refused to appear, two Muslims who were prepared to testify against her, to the cadi's court, and if the case was proven the husband was awarded a certificate exempting him from the necessity of lodging, clothing and maintaining her, and she was thus obliged to find someone else who would, and the long-suffering nearest male relative would be obliged to take her in.

Death, when it visited a member of the family, was not marked by excessive grief; although the departed was mourned there was the comfort of knowing that, as he was a Muslim, his soul had gone to Paradise. A dying man's head was turned towards Mecca and the Declaration of Faith was made on his behalf. The men exclaimed 'Allah, Allah' and the women wailed in their quarters, sometimes with the help of professional mourners. When he died the corpse was washed, the ears, nose and mouth stopped with cotton wool, and the body, ankles tied together and hands laid on his breast, was wrapped in a shroud made of one piece of cloth, without seams. The corpse-washer usually kept the deceased's clothes as a perquisite. The body was buried the same day or the following morning: it was carried from the house on a bier, supported by relays of men, and strangers in the street would share the burden for part of the way as a religious duty. On the bier of a man was laid his turban; on a woman's was placed her head-scarf and perhaps her hair-ornaments and the braids of silk she used to wear with her own hair. The bier was taken to the nearest mosque, where it was placed in the courtyard on a stone kept for that purpose. The imam of the mosque or a close relative recited a prayer for the dead and some Koranic verses, and if the man had been a considerable public figure perhaps also a eulogy. The body was then carried to the place of burial, for preference in the vicinity of the tomb of some venerated personage, and only men followed the procession to the grave. A hole was dug in the ground, and the body, without a coffin, was buried lying on its right side with the head turned towards Mecca. Before the body was covered in, the imam whispered instruction to the deceased on how to answer the questions of the two terrible Examining Angels. A little earth was placed on the corpse, and then a large flat stone laid over it, sometimes with a small shallow cavity to catch rain-water for the birds. Later two upright stones were added at head and foot, with the name, titles and parentage of the deceased; a woman's tombstone bore the name of her father, not her husband. Sometimes a Koranic verse was included, sometimes a more fanciful inscription, such as the stone at Eyub reading:

Well did he know the end of this life, for he had been familiar with its beauties; thinking his appointed time yet another gazelle-eyed one, he said 'My dark-eyed love' and followed it.

It was also customary to carve on the headstone a replica of the turban to which the deceased was entitled during his life; women's gravestones were customarily decorated with sculptured flowers or leaves, or a simple knob. The tombs themselves were never maintained, and no care was given to the grave after the burial, so that as the earth subsided the stones leaned in attitudes of gentle abandon. Cypresses were always planted round about, both because the aromatic resinous scent which they gave off was considered an antidote to the graveyard smells, and because of the implications of immortality in their evergreen leaves. Sometimes, especially on a Friday, a wife would go to sit in their shade and say a prayer for the soul of a departed husband, but generally the graves fell into abandon and disrepair.

37 A tombstone at Eyub, with turban denoting rank of deceased

The death rate was fairly high; even apart from accidents and all those natural ills that the flesh is heir to, there were regular epidemics which swept away a large proportion of the population. Plague was always dormant somewhere in dark corners of the city, especially in military barracks and the foul places around harbours, and outbreaks of malaria were common wherever brackish water and low-lying centres of habitation were exposed to the breeding mosquitoes. There were always some people, particularly the infidels and foreign residents, who attempted to flee the plague, and many residents of Istanbul tried to take refuge on the Prince's Islands because they were cut off from the infected city by water; but this was frequently disastrous since the fierce storms that often raged between the capital and the islands drowned many who thought they were running to safety, and as there were no springs on the islands but only tanks and cisterns to collect the precious rain-water, many of the conditions of comfort remained unfulfilled. The Turkish population was, on the whole, resigned to its fate and appeared unafraid and even reckless in the face of an outbreak of the plague which, at its height, accounted for perhaps 1,000 deaths daily in Istanbul alone.

Although medical services were good, a large number of people both simple and educated had recourse to holy men and wise-women in preference, or as well as, to doctors. Since women were usually in charge of the sick of the household, particularly the children, and since they were on the whole more observant of superstitious practices than the men, they had recourse to many remedies that had very little scientific justification. Babies with convulsions, if they did not respond to mother-of-pearl oil rubbed on the stomach, were frequently exorcised, and the prayers of the night before the end of Ramadan were considered a particularly efficacious cure for insomnia if offered on behalf of a relative or friend. Barrenness, which was considered the greatest disgrace and misfortune that a woman could suffer, was treated by a host of remedies, both magical and medical. Since the Evil Eye was responsible for nine-tenths of all ills, the appeasement of jinns and malevolent spirits, perhaps by blowing on knots, perhaps by the burning of certain hairs or the sweepings of seven shops, or perhaps by the pouring of lead, was frequently resorted to instead of, or before, recourse to more rational medical aid. Much of the medicine administered by holy men and wise-women was, however, homoeopathic in nature, and consequently quite effective. The properties of rhubarb as a laxative and aniseed for the digestion, of an infusion of bitter wood to restore appetite, and the smoking of herbs to relieve congestion in the chest, were widely known, and many brews and ointments made of plants were successfully used.

Many psychological illnesses were often effectively treated by certain groups of professionals who had the exclusive right to practise their particular methods. These practitioners of exorcism and magic, although a greatly feared element in society, were much respected, and fulfilled a vital role. The performances of lead-pourers were especially successful in cases where the patient had been bewitched, that is to say, was in fact psychologically ill. The lead-pourers were an hereditary group of extremely experienced and accredited old women, and much of their success was due to the confidence of both patient and family that they alone had the power to relieve the suffering. Their tools were a melting-ladle, a bowl for water, a towel and the lump of lead which was carried to the patient in a covered basket. After impressive preliminaries the lead was melted in the spoon and poured into the bowl of cold water held above the sufferer's head, which was wrapped in the towel. This procedure was repeated over the patient's navel, over the feet, in the far right corner of the room and over the threshold, the old woman repeating all the while as she melted and poured: 'Not my hand; the hand of our mother Ayesha Fatma.' Some of the water was then given to the patient to drink, and some sprinkled on the head, body and feet. The patient was made to jump three times to and fro over the threshold, a piece of bread was soaked in the water to be taken away and fed to the dogs at the crossroads, and what was left was thrown to the jinns and peris that lurked in the corners of the room. If, when the lead was poured into the water, it fell into bright clean shapes the omens were good, but the treatment could be repeated twice more if necessary, although the old women had to be paid for their services each time. Failure was considered to be due to the overwhelming power of evil in that instance, and the reputation of the lead-pourers remained untarnished. Another, but somewhat less universally respected, group of women operated not with lead but with charcoal embers that had been burned in the household stove.

There were also families known for their ability to set bones, and these were always consulted in the case of broken limbs and even where children were born lame or mis-shapen. Through their hereditary skill, and the experience which they had acquired, some of them achieved extraordinary manipulative powers, and confidence in their ability was fully justified. There were, however, a large number of unskilled and dangerous charlatans practising in all branches of medicine, and desperate women, especially mothers of sick children, provided them with a constant stream of customers. Although it was difficult to prevent people from consulting them privately, they were forbidden by the market inspectors to sit in booths and shops and practise publicly, or to solicit customers, and every now and then they were rounded up and required by the cadi to appear before the Chief Physician, who was head of the medical services throughout the empire, and who examined them for proficiency and, in rare cases, gave them permission to practise.

It was impossible for Muslim women to pass through the same course of medical training as men; nevertheless there were some gifted women who possessed a natural aptitude and soon acquired some experience. If in addition they were able to receive some instruction from a particularly broad-minded man of science, or from some foreign or infidel doctor, they might even become competent to practise surgery on women patients who would not dream of exposing themselves to treatment by a man, or who had been forbidden by their husbands to do so. Indeed, it was probably this total segregation from men, coupled with the dearth of women physicians, that drove so many anxious wives and mothers to seek irrational cures.

There was not on the whole a great deal of mobility between residents of the various quarters, but occasionally, either through fire or rebuilding, or because of the appointment of the head of the household to a post in some other district or town, it became necessary for a family to move house, an occasion of some significance. At the doorway of the new house a sacrifice was made, preferably of a ram whose horns had been painted gold, coat dyed with patches of bright colours, and a ribbon tied around its neck. When its throat had been cut to the accompaniment of the correct invocation, and a little blood had run on the threshold, the animal was taken away and cut up and the meat given to the poor. In a humbler family the sacrifice of a chicken sufficed.

Families always lived in individual units, never in flats or houses shared with other families. The ev, or simple wooden house of the city poor, contained almost no furniture other than mattresses or rugs which were unrolled to make a bed at night, and bundled and stacked against the wall in the daytime. There was also a prayer-mat, a cooking stove and a few pots and spoons, but little else. The floor was of trodden earth, and there was a sink or wash-place in a corner. Food in this sort of household was bought as it was needed, so no storage facilities were necessary. Any changes of clothes were tied in bundles and hung on the wall.

Even in richer houses there was very little free-standing furniture. The most generally popular and useful article was the carpet, which had a variety of uses. Beautiful old ones were hung on the wall for display, the smaller ones woven with the design of a mihrab were used for prayers, others were kept for sleeping on; they were part of the baggage of all travellers. Carpets on the floors of wealthy houses, although of sober colours, were rich and good; since shoes were removed at the door they did not receive a great deal of hard wear. They were spread on top of rush matting, and for coolness in the hottest months they were rolled up and fresh rush mats, finely woven, were laid down for the season.

Both the selamlik and the haremlik, that is, the men's quarters and the women's, had a main reception room, each stepped in the middle so that one half was higher than the other. All around the walls were divans spread with hangings and covered with cushions of velvets and wool fabrics in the winter, and silks and satins in the summer. Here and there on the floor were little square mattresses or heaps of cushions, as occasional seats. The walls and ceiling were painted and carved, and there were niches and shelves for turbans and decorative vases. Here and there about the rooms stood copper or brass mangals, ornate braziers which burned charcoal. As the ceilings were high and there was no glass in the windows, keeping warm in cold weather was a constant preoccupation, and there was no source of heat other than these braziers with their perforated lids which had constantly to be carried out and re-filled with

38 Corner of a reception room, with divan and mangal

glowing embers. In winter the tandur was brought in: a table with a metal foot-rest on which stood a bowl of hot coals, the whole covered with a large quilt. Family and guests sat around it on cushions on the floor, the quilt drawn over their knees and tucked under their arms, or even drawn up to their chins. But even in the richest houses the lighting and heating were on the whole rather crude and inadequate, and also the cause of many small and large domestic fires.

The bedrooms were similar in appearance, except that they had cupboards in the walls to hold bundles of linen and clothes. As in the poorer households, the mattresses and rugs and pillows which were brought out to sleep on at night were rolled up and hidden during the daytime. A bed consisted usually of a mattress stuffed with cotton, about six feet long and four feet wide. This could be placed on a low frame of thongs slung on palm sticks, but as these harboured bed-bugs they were not generally popular. More usually two or three mattresses were piled on top of each other, and, especially to keep children from falling off, long divan cushions were laid down each side. A sheet was spread over both mattress and pillows. In summer people slept almost naked, with only a sheet thrown over them; in the winter they wore as many of their day clothes as they needed to keep warm, and covered themselves with a thick wadded quilt on to which clean top-sheets were pinned. In the hottest parts of the country beds were placed out on the roof-tops in summer.

Almost the only containers in use, both for storing and carrying, were kerchiefs and baskets. Kerchiefs of various sizes and materials held all the types and sizes of clothes, household linen, and every other commodity that could be sorted and tied into bundles and placed in a cupboard. Plain kerchiefs were used to carry clothes and bathing necessities to and from the hammam, embroidered ones for the wrapping of presents; even trays of fruit and sweets sent as gifts were laid on a linen square, with the corners knotted over the top.

In the kitchen and store-rooms, baskets of all kinds held charcoal, vegetables, and indeed all kinds of food, for there were no sacks or wooden tubs or metal containers. In the harem, delicate little baskets of blanched reeds held sweets or coffee-beans or cottons and embroidery silks. Some of the coarser baskets, for heavy duty, were sold at the door by gipsies, who also made circular woven hen-coops, much in demand; others were bought in the Street of the Rush-Workers, where brushes and brooms were also sold. These were made of split reeds, tightly bound at one end and with no handle, so that sweeping and carpet-brushing was always a back-breaking task. Sponges

39 Wall niches, and cupboards for storing bedding in the daytime

were also sold in the basket-makers' street, to be used for washing marble floors, kitchens and fountains, but never for bathing.

The kitchens of big houses stood in a separate building in the court-yard, so that the cooking smells and heat should not offend the family. The work was done in brick ovens and over large shallow troughs of charcoal. There was also a small kitchen in the harem in which the women prepared for themselves any little dishes that they fancied, or engaged in making the particular jams and preserves which were the pride of that household. In addition to this kind of activity, the lady of the house also supervised the cleaning, and herself dusted or washed the valuable pieces of porcelain. As women seldom received much education, only a few might be able to read a little and recite all or part of the Koran. They could knit, sew and embroider, but life in the harem was idle and boring with such limited activities. They seldom participated in any of the entertainments and festivities that took place outdoors in the course

111

of the year, and a great deal of time was spent in gossip, and in peering through the heavily shuttered windows àt the life passing outside. For this reason, although large houses had their own separate bath-houses for men and women they did not replace the social visits to the haṁmam.

These visits, free from the repressive authority of menfolk, took place usually once a week in both winter and summer, and were occasions for meetings with friends and strangers, exchange of news, inspection of potential daughters-in-law and of their own daughters' rivals. Mothers of sons were superior to the mothers of daughters and took precedence over them as centres of gossip. Usually all the women of the household went to the hammam together, taking all they required for the day, including food and refreshments; they also brought their embroidery or knitting or any small work they were engaged on. Sometimes the accompanying maid would scrub the private washroom three times while the mistress's party waited for it to be done to her satisfaction.

40 Woman and girl attendant in the hammam

Hammam procedure was to wash three times, then have a meal, then a nap or gossip as they sat over their handwork in the cool room, and then three washes again before the bundles were finally packed up. During the washing periods, superfluous hair was removed with a depilatory paste made of quicklime and orpiment, applied with a spatula and removed with the razor-sharp edge of a mussel shell; the skin was scrubbed with a coarse bag over the hand; the soles of the feet were rubbed with rasps; the hair washed with yolk of egg and the white applied round the eyes as a corrective for wrinkles; perfumes and oils were tried and exchanged. There were no bath-like containers in which bathers could sit and wash, for there was a strong distaste for what they considered still water, but all round the walls hot water gushed out of copper spouts into little marble basins, to be

41 Cooling-room in the men's hammam

splashed around and thrown over the body with the little brass bowls they had brought with them. High wooden pattens, sometimes inlaid with mother-of-pearl or beautifully ornamented with silver, were worn to keep them from slipping on the wet marble floors. Dark corners of hammams were a particular lurking-place of envious jinns, and the special precautions necessary in those places were never omitted.

Although women made such a great family outing of their trips to the hammam, men in fact went even more often, although generally alone or with one or two friends. When the bather arrived his clothes were put in a shawl with the corners tied, and he sat smoking on his divan waiting until his masseur called him to be kneaded and massaged, scrubbed with a glove and washed. The less wealthy customers did not employ the barbers, masseurs and washers who were attached to the hammams, but bought their depilatory from pedlars at the door and removed their beards themselves. There were also ambulant barbers who hung around hammams and who would trim the hair and beard while the customer sat on a little rush stool which they carried under their arms. The atmosphere generally was one of calm relaxation, although there were a few men's baths, especially in the cities, with an extremely evil reputation. As with the women's baths, some were reserved for infidels but others received infidels only on certain days and at times fixed by the market inspector, and the razors, towels and other articles for their use were kept separate from those of Muslims.

Visits between families, usually on the part of the women, were another distraction. These too lasted all day and the husbands of both visitor and hostess seldom intruded on these occasions. The party of women went from one house to the other attended by servants, and if they were obliged to walk it was considered bad manners to stare at them. During these visits news was shared and gossip exchanged, children compared, matches discussed and trousseaux examined, and sweets, fruit and drinks supplied continuously.

Picnic parties, which usually included the children and often the master of the household, were another all-day outing. Sometimes in Istanbul the trip was made by water, in one or more caiques hired to take the party to a favourite spot along the Bosphorus or up the Golden Horn. More often the men rode on horses or mules and the women travelled sitting on the floor of large slow ox-carts, pulled by a pair of the lumbering beasts decorated with high arched rods of wood from which hung thick red woollen tassels. However hot the day these carts were always heavily draped to conceal the women from the eyes of strangers. At the picnic-place the women and the younger children of the party would, as at home, sit apart from the men, perhaps on the other side of the fountain, and the servants or young girls would unpack the food; but however much they had brought with them they always bought some tempting

42 Ox-cart with picnic party

delicacy from the pedlars who gathered near them—rice-jelly sprinkled with rose-water and cut into squares on its tray with a brass shovel, fruit-soup with ice floating in it, lokoum with nuts, or sherbet poured through a lump of snow stuck over the spout of the ewer. An itinerant musician played, the women chattered, and the menfolk would so far unbend as to play with the children in public, for nothing brought the Turkish soul so much ease and contentment as the contemplation of nature.

Many upper-class women were called on by shop-keepers or brokers in their own home if they wished to purchase some particular object, and indeed the women brokers who circulated among rich houses on behalf of jewellers and silk- or fur-merchants were often also very useful matchmakers, since they knew the composition of so many households. On a very few occasions, however, some women went out to shop, attended by their slaves and eunuchs, and as these excursions were so rare they took the greatest delight in turning everything in the shop upside-down before determining on the exquisite pair of slippers, or whatever it might be that pleased them.

Whatever the excursion, however, whether alone or with their men-folk, the women were always home by sunset. It would have been quite unthinkable that any of them should be on the street after dark.

Poorer women had less time to be bored, for they were kept very busy at home. They made almost everything which the family wore, prepared all the food, reared the children and, outside the towns, worked on the land as well.

Family evenings, particularly when there were guests, were spent with great formality and dignity, the women being received, apart as always, in the haremlik. There the hostess, and other women of the family and any guests, sat on the divan or mattresses, the family retainers sitting below the step and the high-ranking maids by the wall near the door. The evening was spent in conversation, reading or embroidery; when the senior maid brought in the refreshments of sweetmeats, sherbet and fresh and dried fruits all the ladies partook, although the maids sat a little apart and ate very sparingly. Evenings in the selamlik were passed in grave conversation, the servants standing silent around the walls, arms crossed on their breasts and hands concealed in the sleeves.

Servants and slaves were adopted very intimately into the household, but good manners kept all relationships within bounds, particularly on formal occasions and in the presence of outsiders. They fell into various categories; highest in status was the beslemeh. She was an adopted girl— and the adoption of children as a charitable duty was not uncommon —who was the child of a poor family and was taken into a more fortunate though not necessarily very wealthy household. Although theoretically the girl was to be treated as an adopted daughter, and a husband found for her, in fact it very often happened that she became an esteemed but unpaid servant, perhaps one of the kalfas who sat below the step. Other servants of the household, cooks, grooms and door-keepers, were all free to change their employment whenever they wished, although usually there existed a very high degree of loyalty to the family. Slaves, on the other hand, could be bought, sold, hired, loaned or given. In addition to his four statutory wives a man might, for example, have as many female slaves as he wished to be his concubines, although he had no right to any of his wife's female slaves. If a concubine bore her master a child she could not thereafter be sold or given away, and if he did not give her her freedom immediately she was entitled to it at his death; the child, if he acknowledged it as his own—and he usually did—was free at once. An owner was not allowed to marry one of his own slaves, although he could give either a male or female slave away in marriage to anyone else, slave or free. Often an intelligent, loyal slave, skilled in the owner's business, was married to a daughter of the house and made a completely acceptable son-in-law. All the women servants and slaves were part of the harem, under the authority of the senior lady, whose duty it was to keep the squabbles and jealousies, that inevitably arose, from troubling the master of the house. The male servitors lived in the selamlik, and usually slept on a mat on the floor in their day-clothes in the small rooms round the open courtyard under the house and covered in bad weather with a cloak or blanket. Only the very wealthiest families could afford to have eunuchs, who passed freely between the two divisions of the household.

Except on ceremonial occasions the food in Turkish houses was very simple and the drink was water, and little time was spent on eating. The master of the house, if he had no guests, would sometimes choose to eat with his wife and children in the harem, and he was always served first, either by his wife or by a servant. The family stood around him, and no one would sit or take a mouthful until he had begun and given them permission to join him. The dietary laws had few but rigid taboos, which forbade the eating of any animal that had not been slaughtered 'In the name of God'; its throat cut near the head, severing the windpipe, gullet and carotid arteries. It was forbidden also to eat animals found already dead, or the meat of pigs.

Breakfast, which was taken very early in the morning just after the dawn prayer, consisted for the poor of bread, curd cheese, olives and, especially in cold weather, soup. The wealthier had white cheese, fruit, jams and preserves with bread, and drank glasses of tea. The main cooking for the evening meal was done in the afternoon, and lunch at home consisted of what was left from the day before. The poorer people ate a great deal of onion and garlic to flavour their coarse bread, as well as sheepsheads and tripe and the other offal of those beasts who supplied the rich with meat. Cheap vegetables made their thick soups, and rice was their staple starch; milk and buffalo yoghurt were popular and inexpensive, and these foods were consumed with dispatch in the late afternoon when they came home from work. Artisans and labourers who could not get home for lunch took a little helva, or an onion and a piece of bread tied in a kerchief, and this, with a little water, was their midday meal. Those who sent out for food from the cookshop usually had a dish of stew and a little rice, or else some milk dish such as rice-flour pudding, or junket from the pedlar with the tray of bowls on his head.

In better homes, and particularly if there were guests, the evening meal consisted of several dishes of pilaffs, soups and stews, always served consecutively and in quick succession. Everybody washed before all meals, particularly the right hand which was reserved for clean occupations, especially eating. A tray was brought in and placed on a low stool to form a table. It was laid with spoons and metal plates, or with large flat pieces of bread, either leavened or unleavened, which were used as plates and themselves consumed at the end of the meal. The diners sat on the floor round the tray, the right knee raised and the left flat on the ground, and in this way as many as twelve people could sit round a 'table' three feet wide. The right arm was bared to the elbow and the hanging end of sleeve tucked up, and each diner had a napkin or shared a long narrow towel draped round to cover everyone's lap. The master of the house said 'Bismillah'—'In the name of God'—and the meal began.

43 *Men at dinner*

Spoons were only used for soup and other liquids; all other food was picked up in the fingers, and for this reason it was always prepared in pieces of suitable size, and large joints of meat, or fowl, were served boned and so well cooked that they were easily broken up at the table. To eat rice, a portion was taken from the dish between the thumb and fingers and pressed into a wad, to be conveyed neatly to the mouth. Water, or sometimes sherbet, was drunk at the end of the meal. Great decorum was observed throughout: fingers were never licked, there was no belching or lip-smacking. Then the hands were washed again under water poured, by the wife or a servant, from a tall ewer into a copper bowl with a perforated cover.

All Turks, and indeed all Muslims, had a great taste for sweet things, but these were never eaten with the meal except at wedding parties and banquets. The sweetening was provided by honey or a thick molasses made from grape sugar, called pekmez, and these and a variety of flavourings were used for dozens of sweet dishes and pastries, sometimes served with thick heavy buffalo cream and eaten at any time of the day, both in the selamlik and the haremlik.

In larger households food was stored according to the season, and tremendous supplies were laid in, in the autumn, of the season's oil, onions, honey and pekmez, preserved meats and fish, pickles and jams and fruit syrups, rice and cracked wheat and flour, nuts and dried fruits and cheeses. Fat-tailed sheep provided lard for cooking as well as oil for lamps, and baskets of fuel for the stoves and fodder for the animals were stacked in the courtyard. In the spring and summer an enormous variety of fresh fruit and vegetables and salads were available in Istanbul, where food from all corners of the empire was both cheap and plentiful, and in many other towns; in the country the variety was limited by the local quality of the soil and standard of husbandry, as well as by the very low gastronomic standard and the scant social importance attached to meals.

Whatever one's resources, however, the entertainment of a guest was a sacred duty, no matter how unexpected his arrival. Food and drink, of the best that could be provided, were at once offered, as well as a bed if the visit were protracted, and while he was under the family roof the guest's needs and preferences were accorded overriding importance. If, when he left, he had a considerable way to go, he was supplied with food for the journey.

Casual visitors, no matter how familiar with the family, would in no circumstances enter a house unannounced, or without calling 'Destur' to warn the ladies of the household to retreat into the harem. A certain formality characterised the social relationships of all classes, and even the conventions of greeting were rigidly observed. Thus, a person riding saluted a man on foot, a man walking by greeted those sitting or standing still, a small party gave the first salutation to a larger party, the young to the old, the one entering a house to those within. Between Muslims the greeting was 'Peace be on you', and the reply 'On you be peace, and the mercy of God and His blessings', both said with the right hand on the breast, or raised to lips and forehead. Within the household, a son kissed his father's hand, a wife her husband's, and a slave or servant his master's, or, to show great humility, the sleeve or hem of his robe.

It was the observance of these and many other conventions of behaviour and manners that gave such solemnity to the pace of public life; their civilising effects combined with the innate humanity of the Turkish character to bring dignity as well as pattern to their domestic life.

6

The Course of the Year

The Turkish day was divided into two twelve-hour periods and began at sunset; one hour after sunset was, therefore, one o'clock, and twelve hours after was considered to be the end of the night. They then began to count the hours of day, concluding at the 12 o'clock sunset. The year had 354 days, made up of six lunar months of thirty days and six of twenty-nine, which meant that it was eleven days shorter than the solar year, and fixed annual events rotated through the seasons eleven days earlier each year. Year 1 of the Muslim era was AD 622, the year of the Prophet's *Hijra*, his migration from Mecca to Medina. Useful almanacs were issued annually: long narrow rolls of vellum divided into columns which showed the hours of prayer, the solar and lunar months and days, the phases of the moon, sunrise and sunset, as well as such general information as the dates of Greek festivals. They also included a list of days fortunate and unfortunate for a variety of enterprises; for example in 1593 the 9th day of Safer, the second month, was propitious for inviting people to dinner, the 12th unfavourable for the submission of petitions to the Sultan, the 16th unlucky for travelling and the 18th for buying horses. But the pattern and rhythm of Turkish life was essentially regulated by the succession of religious and secular festivals that punctuated the year, and by the passage of the seasons with their appropriate tasks and rewards. Even the main divisions of the working day were marked by the hours of prayer, which were for most people adequate guides to time-keeping; a man's working year could be interrupted by a seven-months' absence on pilgrimage, or any army might return from campaign in time to help with the harvest, and this very flexibility occurred within a context of timeless and reassuring continuity.

The year began with the month of Muharrem, and was ushered in without much ceremony: contemporaries exchanged greetings and the young kissed the hands of the old, who gave them a coin which was kept all year for luck. But the first ten days of Muharrem were also the first of the great religious holy days, and the tenth day in particular was observed with prayers and lamentations commemorating the death of the martyr Huseyn, and a special dish, called Ashure, was eaten. This was made by members of the Sunni sect with seven ingredients and by Shiites with twelve, and always included nuts, raisins and other dried fruit boiled with cereals; although the number was of religious symbolism the ingredients were also popularly associated with the depleted supplies which Noah found in his stores after the safe landing of the Ark, and which he mixed together to make a celebratory meal. Throughout the ten days the blind beggars who wandered about the streets were the particular recipients of alms.

The next great event of the year, eagerly awaited, was the return at the beginning of Rebi I, the third month, of the pilgrims who had departed for Mecca months before. Although there were some early arrivals and a few late stragglers, the party usually travelled together for protection, and friends and relatives went out to greet them and kiss their hands and accompany them home. Everybody sought the pilgrim's blessing and intercession, and strangers in the street would beg him to touch them and say 'God, pardon him'. Houses were decorated, the pilgrim's door was painted green, and on the threshold prayers of thanksgiving were recited together with the pious wish that others would soon be able to make the blessed journey. On the day after his return the holy Zemzem water which the pilgrim had brought back was set out in the finest receptacle the house could provide, and as visitors arrived to welcome him they were offered little dishes of food and, specifically, small square mouthfuls of fried dough dipped in heavy syrup, which kept at least one woman in the household unremittingly busy over the fire. The celebration lasted for three days, during which the small gifts from the holy city were distributed among his womenfolk and friends: kohl for darkening the eyes, tied in little bags made of red aloes bark, rings and trinkets, and little cakes of the wonder-working earth of Mecca. Families came also to enquire for any news of their own pilgrims who had not yet returned, for many died during the journey. The party which returned to Istanbul brought with it the letter of greeting to the Sultan from the Sherīf of Mecca, who was the senior representative of the House of the Prophet. This was delivered with great solemnity into the hands of the Grand Vizier, to be read in the mosque in the Sultan's presence on the commemoration of the birthday of the Prophet. This followed closely, on the 12th day of Rebi I, and was celebrated as a religious festival.

In the course of the year, besides a number of holy days, some of which were celebrated with rejoicing and public festivities, there were seven holy nights marked by devout prayer and deeply impressive religious chanting, and no other manifestation except the illumination of the interiors of the mosques and the galleries of the minarets. The first of these nights fell on the eve of the Prophet's birthday; then followed on the first Thursday in Rejeb, the seventh month, the eve of his conception;

on the 27th night, the anniversary of his miraculous journey to heaven and return to earth. Next, the 15th night of Shaban, the eighth month, was the Night of Justification, when the recording angels summarised the lives of men and the Angel of Death opened a new register in which were inscribed the names of those destined to die within the year. The most dread and mysterious of all was the Night of Power, the 27th night of the ninth month, Ramadan, which celebrated the revelation of the Koran to Muhammad, and in which all nature, animate and inanimate, acknowledged the greatness of God. Rare was the believer who did not participate in the night prayers; throughout the country, in the great royal mosques of Istanbul as in the humblest village, thousands of Muslims swayed, knelt and chanted, moving devoutly as one man. On this night, it was generally believed, the destinies of the true believers were drawn up for the following year. The last night of Ramadan, and the eve of the Day of Sacrifice which fell on the 10th of Zilhijje, the twelfth month of the year, were also observed with piety. On these seven nights men were forbidden any communication with their harem, except that on the Night of Power the Sultan visited the bed of a selected slave girl, and if a baby ensued it was considered a symbol of the glory and prosperity of the house of Osman.

During the seventh month all those who proposed to participate in the pilgrimage of the year congregated at centres of departure. The largest party from Turkey left Istanbul on the 12th of Rejeb, and a ceremonial procession round the town preceded their departure. The Sultan was represented by proxies, and he sent large gifts of treasure, partly as a donation to the holy cities to be used for the relief of the poor in their neighbourhood, and partly to be given as protection-money to the savage Bedouin tribesmen who beset the pilgrims' path. On the pommel of his horse the Sultan's envoy carried a gold-embroidered green case in which was a silk bag containing a letter of compliment and greeting to the Sherīf of Mecca. The greatest feature of the procession was the appearance in the royal caravan of two holy camels, of antique pedigree, which were used for no mundane purpose during the rest of the year. The first camel was gorgeously caparisoned, and on its back it carried a high pinnacled litter, the mahmil, which travelled to Mecca as the symbol of the Sultan's political authority. The animal was hung with rich cloths that amost hid it completely. The second camel bore only a saddle of green velvet and silver, in shape like that of the Prophet's own saddle. On their appearance there was a great stir in the crowd: men murmured 'Allah, Allah', and some of the simpler people bowed deeply as they passed. The camels were followed by a train of grooms and attendants and hundreds of beasts of burden carrying the treasure and supplies, and the tent-cloths and poles with which protective coverings were erected every night for the mahmil and the Sultan's letter. A large military escort also accompanied the party to act as protection along the way, and also to supply detachments for the annual relief of the garrisons that lay on the route. When the caravan was ready to depart, all those who, having made provision for their family left behind and preparation for the journey before them, were ready for the pilgrimage, said a last goodbye to their families and friends and joined the procession which wound through the city to Sirkeji, crossed the water to Uskudar, and started on the long road to Mecca.

Although the Night of Power was the most holy of the year, the observance of Ramadan lasted throughout the lunar month which bore its name, and was the most taxing and revealing of the religious festivals. It partook of the solemnity of religious observance, the rigours of self-discipline and the

44 The mahmil

indulgence of unusual distractions during the hours of release. In addition to the fasting and prayers that occupied the days, Ramadan was the occasion of a number of other religious observances. On the 15th day, for example, the Sultan and the senior dignitaries of the state paid homage to the relics of the Prophet, which consisted of his battle standard, his mantle, the hairs of his beard, his footprint set in a piece of rock and two of his teeth. The ceremony of uncovering and displaying these relics, and their veneration, occurred after the midday prayer; it was an occasion of great general religious significance even though it was conducted in respectful privacy. During the second half of Ramadan other relics in the care of various custodians were publicly displayed, and part of the offerings of money made by the devout who visited them was used by the guardians for the proper maintenance of the shrines. Ramadan also provided certain secular anniversaries: on the day after the Night of Power the cloth warehouse in Istanbul was opened and the chiefs of the 162 companies of Janissaries arrived with their men. There, under the supervision of the Chief of the Janissaries, the Aghas and the heads of the depôt, the men marched up, a company at a time, to collect their allowance of muslin for turbans and cambric for shirts, and the lengths of blue Salonika cloth to be made up later into uniforms by official tailors in the two great state workshops.

The sacred month had been preceded by preparations which were an upset and an excitement to the whole household. The store-rooms of the houses were crammed with food and even the poorest took in provisions, and extra servants were hired in the big houses. The day's fast was traditionally broken by various foods, sometimes a handful of raisins, sometimes a drink of apricot paste mixed with water, but the first meal of the evening was everywhere a feast, and the announcement at sunset, by drum and cannon and muezzin, of the evening prayer and the end of the day's rigours and rituals, was also the signal for the beginning of an evening's private and public festivities such as took place at no other time of the year.

Ramadan was the exception, too, to the general practice of being within doors after nightfall. Every night of the month the minarets were encircled with lights, the streets were illuminated and the cafés open and, when they had eaten, men passed freely about the streets enjoying the full and varied night life available at no other time of the year. Some of the entertainments were religious in character, and the most popular of these were recitals of the Koran by celebrated hafizes who would chant in turn for hours throughout the night. These had been hired for the occasion by very wealthy families, and performed usually in the outer courtyards of palaces and mansions. The gates were always left open and any passer-by was free to join the audience, squatting on the floor or on low benches around the walls. There, by the light of flares, enraptured by the rise and fall of the chant of the voices, sat soldiers, hammals and beggars side by side with pashas, beys and senior ecclesiastics, all equal in participation.

45 *Hajivat and Karagöz*

Of the less exalted popular amusements none was perhaps more typical of the Ramadan night entertainments than the performances of the puppet shadow theatre, Karagöz, which took place both in coffee-houses and in rich private homes. Every quarter had its Karagöz, and the making and manipulating of the puppets was an extremely skilled craft. A master in this art was identified by the number of tassels which were hung over the middle of his screen, and the chief of their guild was chosen from among those entitled to seven tassels, as were those selected to perform before the Sultan, for Karagöz was as popular in the Palace as in the cafés.

The Karagöz characters were figures about 15 inches high, oiled to make them translucent, and coloured; the best were made of camel-skin, which was less inclined to buckle and warp, but horse- and calf-skin were also used although they were more opaque and generally less successful. The principal characters were Karagöz and Hajivat, representing the simple but cunning man-in-the-street and the educated fellow who gave himself airs, but there were many others, caricaturing a variety of races, professions and religions. They were jointed, with waxed thread at the neck, arms, waist and knees, and were manipulated from the back by rods held between the fingers. Complete sets of all the figures required for the performance of a play were displayed for sale, hung by a string through the eyes, in the booth of the craftsman who made them. The background and scenery, sometimes of quite complicated objects such as moving ships, swaying palm-trees and writhing dragons, were similarly made and jointed. The Karagöz theatre consisted of a three-sided booth covered by a curtain printed with branches and roses, with a white cotton screen about three feet by four feet inserted across the front. On a wooden shelf behind the screen stood a large flat bowl of iron or copper filled with oil and with a thick cotton wick. Inside was coiled a heavy chain to absorb the heat. The performance was introduced by a two- or three-man orchestra who sat at the foot of a small raised stage and played until the audience had arrived and settled down; each puppet and theme had an identifying melody which recurred throughout the performance and the orchestra provided these too. When the puppet-master judged that the time was ready he lit the oil lamp, which was the signal that brought the audience to attention, and as the coloured shadow appeared of a tree with shaking fruit, or a witch, or a wrestler fighting a seven-headed monster, or as perhaps a ship in full sail or a rider on horseback passed across the stage, they fell silent. In addition to moving the puppets the manipulator spoke all their parts in various voices, sang songs, made a variety of sound-effects, and into the old, familiar and well-loved plots he introduced a number of improvised comic scenes, sometimes of current or local interest, which included a great deal of ribaldry and a number of coarse jokes. Separate and sedater performances were sometimes given for women and children, who otherwise might watch from behind curtains and screens if the room in which the performance took place were suitable.

There was also a live popular theatre which performed in the open air.

An area about 25 yards by 30 was cleared, and a small stage was roped off in the middle, around which the audience sat, knelt or stood. Near the entrance sat a small orchestra who played at the beginning while the minor characters danced round the stage to entertain the waiting audience, and who introduced each character with an identifying tune as he appeared during the performance. They also played between episodes, although there was no complete break and the actors remained on the stage beating time with their feet to the interval music. The stage set always consisted of a low screen with a chair in front of it, representing a shop, and a higher two-leaved screen for other scenes. There were, of course, no female performers; male actors took all the women's parts, which were generally less important. The themes were familiar, and the two major characters, Pishekar, the man of the world—who was usually also an adept conjuror—and Kavuklu, the comic, introduced the various episodes in the form of the re-telling of stories or dreams. These were then enacted, and always contained a great many comic dances, jingles, contemporary allusions and knock-about humour. There were also always the extremely popular caricature imitations of stock figures: the stupid peasant Turk, the cunning Jew and Armenian, the simpleton Frank, and the exaggeratedly incomprehensible refinements of the upper-class Ottomans. These theatres had, understandably, an enormous following, although it was perhaps not so totally classless as that of the Karagöz. The Greeks and Armenians also had a repertory theatre and, as they had no objection to women performers who sang and danced unveiled on the stage, they were also visited with guilty pleasure by Turkish theatre-goers who were deeply smitten by these exposed faces.

Neither the Karagöz nor the live theatre appeared exclusively at the time of Ramadan, and the mimes and professional story-tellers were an even more familiar sight, but they too came into their own on these nights. The less famous, and the itinerants who went round the villages, often performed in public squares, but usually the story-teller sat on a cushioned stool on a small raised platform in the coffee-house or boza shop, or, in warmer weather, against the wall outside. The café-owner gave him a small fee for attracting custom, in addition to the collections of money that were made for him several times in the course of his long recital, but even those who had no money to spend in the coffee-houses were admitted to sit in the corner and listen. On a small table before him lay the scarf and wand which were the emblems of his profession. Sometimes he was attended by musicians who accompanied him when he chanted poetry, or played the prelude and interludes to his tales; sometimes he accompanied himself on a one-stringed fiddle. There were some story-tellers who read aloud from books, or who recited stories from books that they had learned by heart, about legendary Muslim heroes; others, particularly the story-tellers from Erzerum, told these epics as they had

46 Story-teller

been handed down by word of mouth, with their own musical accompaniment; while a third group, from Istanbul, told folk stories and traditional tales in a variety of voices, including extremely clever female impersonations, sometimes interspersed with the playing of a tune to give them some respite. When their voices were rested and they were ready to go on with the story they set aside their instruments and tapped on the table with their wand to bring the assembly to order.

47 *Nasreddin Hoja, depicted, as usual, on his donkey*

The most famous character of these popular tales was Nasreddin Hoja, the thirteenth-century imam, teacher and homespun philosopher on whom most traditional Turkish jokes were fathered. A typical story, which would be told mainly in direct speech in an assortment of voices and with suitable cries and groans, was of Nasreddin Hoja awakened one night by the shouts of two men quarrelling in front of his house. He wrapped himself in his quilt and ran outside to separate the men who had now come to blows, but they, resenting his interference, rounded on him and beat him unmercifully, finally running off with his quilt. Bruised and aching, Nasreddin Hoja returned wearily to his room, and his wife asked sleepily what the men had been quarrelling about. 'About my quilt, apparently,' he replied, 'because they've got it and they've stopped quarrelling.' In another story, Nasreddin Hoja was invited to a feast, but turning up in his everyday clothes he was scorned by the other guests and insolently treated by the servants. He slipped away to his home and returned in a fine fur coat, and was then treated with deference and seated in a place of honour. Thereupon he took a spoonful of soup, and dripping it slowly on to his coat he said loudly and clearly: 'Eat, my coat, eat! You were the one who was really invited here, not I.' There were thousands of Nasreddin Hoja stories, but even the repetitions of old favourites were made fresh by the talents of these masters.

Some of the greatest entertainers, who commanded high fees, were equally skilled in manipulation of the Karagöz, in imitations, recitations and in fact all forms of these performing arts.

There were also a number of dancing-boys and girls, who belonged to several rival troupes, and were hired out as professional entertainers to give exhibitions of dancing in public cafés or private houses. Both boy and girl dancers were called by the same name—chengi—and the boys were generally more in demand than the girls. They wore their hair in long ringlets and they dressed like girls and performed suggestive dances, marking time with finger-snapping or small instruments such as wooden spoons or pairs of wooden sticks which they clicked together. The admiring audience would spit on coins and stick them to the dancers' faces, especially their foreheads, as they moved around among them. Some of these dancing-boys became extremely famous and were the cause of many jealous fights, especially among Janissaries in the taverns. When the boys lost their looks and their beards began to grow they abandoned their dancing and became drummers and trainers to other dancing boys, for preparation could be extremely rigorous. Some were taught precise movements of head, arms and feet, and were suspended in baskets from the ceiling which were spun around very fast to accustom them to the movement of whirling; others specialised in pantomime dances with mimics playing such conventional rôles as tax-collectors and street vendors. The better-class troupes were highly trained to perform for a very discriminating private clientèle, and a group of these dancing boys was attached to the Serai. The girls also performed provocative dances, in the course of which they would kneel and lean back, continuing their rhythmic movements, until their heads touched the floor, when they too would have coins stuck on their foreheads by the enthusiastic audience; but these performances were generally regarded as improper and unsuitable for people of more refined tastes. Among the dancers were many troupes of Greeks, Armenians, Jews and gypsies, and there was such jealousy and rivalry between the groups that street quarrels, sometimes very unpleasant but sometimes also a source of vulgar entertainment, would break out.

48 Dancing-boy, clicking wooden sticks to mark the beat

There was a popular form of spectacle which lasted for about three hours, often found in the more unsophisticated small towns. This consisted sometimes simply of music with instruments and songs, sometimes of

49 Javelin-throwing, on the meadows at Kagithane

dancing in which both boys and girls performed and which included some grotesque capers by the company wearing masks and painted caps: a third variety was one of speech entertainment, including poetry-reading, joke-telling and imitations. The most favoured combination was one of music, dance and drama, and in all circumstances the performance was always concluded with a prayer of thanksgiving.

Many booths appeared in the streets, offering a variety of small distractions. The snake-charmers, many of them dervishes, not only ate scorpions as well as serpents, but also demonstrated how they carried those insects live in their caps next to their shaven heads. Particularly in demand on these evenings were the fortune-tellers' booths. The lower orders favoured the method in which the seer used a roughly outlined picture of some legendary hero or a mythological character. In response to the question posed by the customer he would study the picture with great concentration, and when the revelation of the answer had come to him he would expound it in humorous couplets. According to another highly respected method, more common in the eastern provinces, the left palm of a young virgin boy was cupped to hold a pool of black ink into which the fortune-teller would gaze raptly until, possibly through self-induced hypnotism, he began to speak in an unfamiliar voice, fore-telling the future of the enquirer or describing occasions and events occurring at the moment miles away. Some fortune-tellers were simply-equipped, with a small bag made of gazelle-skin which held a few shells, pieces of coloured glass, small coins, and perhaps a few beans. They would shake the bag, throw the contents on the ground, and read the future from the shapes that emerged and the proximity of one object to another. These 'prophets' also undertook tattooing. There were sword-

swallowers, fire-eaters, magicians, and troupes of jugglers and tumblers, acrobats who might turn up at the summer picnic-places to climb a greasy pole or walk a tight-rope across a river, or provide the diversion at some circumcision feast, but who could certainly be counted on to make their appearance at Ramadan.

But after the night's diversions, and well before the morning prayer, the drums reminded the faithful that it was time to take the last meal, usually the rice dish called pilaff that would lie heavy on their stomachs and sustain them, and with the dawn prayer began another day of abstinence and lenten solemnity. Often towards the end of the month tempers became short from the enforced self-control and lack of sleep, friends fell out or street-fights flared up, and there was relief when the end of Ramadan was signalled by the sight of the new moon. Once again the mosques were full that night for prayers of thanksgiving. The next day was celebrated with devotions and the giving of alms, but also the new clothes which had been made ready before the beginning of the holy month were brought out and proudly worn during the exchange of visits. Everybody gave gifts of sweets tied in kerchiefs decorated with spangles, and the day was in fact called 'Sugar Holiday', and was one of the happiest of the year, with the greatest air of joyfulness about it. Throughout the empire there were celebrations in squares and parks, on land and on water, and also many spectator sports. The principal of these was javelin-throwing, which was played by teams of men on horseback: the object was to throw lances, about ten feet long, at the back or head of members of the opposing team in such a way as to dislodge them from their mounts. This was a great favourite in the countryside, where villages or tribes contested hotly with each other and spectators peered

50 Archer

through the dust of the flying hooves and cheered the custodians of their honour. Archery was a national sport whose champions became folk heroes, and displays of skill drew spectators from miles around. Contests included the longest flight of an arrow, and commemorative stelae were erected to mark record distances; also, shooting at such minute targets as distant bottles, mirrors, lanterns, or a gilded apple on top of a tall mast. Another showy trick was to shoot an arrow and catch it in the hand as it fell, or to shoot more than one at a time. Since, unlike the infantry bowmen of the west, these archers were mounted, they used the short bow of central Asia. These, and most other sports, including wrestling with oiled bodies, mace-swinging and polo, were in fact forms of military exercise, and their practice contributed to prowess on the battlefield. Until the beginning of the sixteenth century Turks rode the tough Tatar horses, but these were then supplanted by the swift Arab breed; the grooms who had the custody of these valuable animals were usually Arabs or Berbers, and the horse trade was almost entirely in the hands of gipsy dealers, who had one of the wealthiest guilds in the country.

Hunting-parties were a feature of this day, although the chase after game was general throughout the year, as much for food as for sport. Larger game was trapped and sent to the towns to be fattened and used for meat, and birds were hunted mainly for their plumes: cranes' feathers were used for the parade head-dresses of the Janissaries, herons' feathers for imperial aigrettes, and goose and pigeon feathers for the flights of arrows. Nightingales and other song birds were caught to hang in cages in reception rooms, although it was considered a pious duty at Ramadan to buy cage-birds and give them their freedom. Other game was pursued on horseback and on foot, with dogs, hunting-leopards and falcons, and the Sultan's huntsmen, too, were part of the military forces: certain companies of soldiers were known as the Mastiffers, the Falconers, the Craners, and by other similar titles. The Sultan himself usually practised a variety of sports, and competed at the famous archery field at Okmeydan, while the palace pages were also trained to participate in most of them.

The last holy day of the year was the Day of Sacrifice, the 10th of Zilhijje, the twelfth month, which was not accompanied by any merry-making. It expressed the identification of those at home with the pilgrims to Mecca, who had reached that point of their journey which required a sacrifice on Mount Arafat, and they demonstrated their participation by performing a similar act. Flocks of sheep and goats were brought from Rumelia and Anatolia and waited on the outskirts of the towns. Thousands were massed on the hills round Istanbul, and some even in streets and squares, their horns gilded, their fleeces washed, combed, dyed with henna and decorated with ribbons, amulets and paper banners. As many families as could afford it bought one of these animals to be sacrificed, its throat cut as its head was turned towards Mecca and, as an act of piety, its meat given to the poor. The less well-off sacrificed whatever animal they could afford and ate the meat themselves.

There were certain occasions, not all of them festive, which the Sultan ordered to be generally observed. The processions which preceded the departure of the army on campaign were a most impressive spectacle, accompanied by the firing of cannon, the beating of drums and performances by the military bands, and the populace turned out in force. The Sultan, who alone had the right to perform this office, brought out 'the Prophet's standard which, with his other holy relics, were guarded wrapped in forty silken coverings in the mihrab of the hall near the throne-room. The standard accompanied the Sultan or the Grand Vizier into battle, and as it passed through the streets, either on the departure of the army or its return, men bowed and touched the ground before it, murmuring in awe, 'Allah, Allah'. At its safe return prayers were said and incense of aloes and ambergris was burned around it; the home-coming of the victorious army was, of course, celebrated with the most tremendous rejoicing.

The girding of the Sultan, the formal acknowledgment of his accession, was marked by a public holiday, as were other royal, commemorative or patriotic occasions such as the birth or circumcision of the Sultan's children, the wedding of a member of the royal family or some other great

51 Men lighting fireworks for a display. The spectators watch from a safe distance, while firemen stand by with skins of water

marriage, the triumph of a famous warrior, the arrival of a foreign ambassador or visitor of note whom the court wished particularly to honour. The Sultan usually made a generous contribution for the pro-

134

vision of entertainments, which included spectacular pageants, mock battles between Muslims and Christians, water triumphs, illuminations and fireworks.

Frequently, additional entertainment was furnished by the guilds, who mounted a procession of tableaux which displayed their trade techniques. The greatest of these processions consisted of the heads of the military, naval and civil establishments with detachments of troops, senior members of the clergy, representatives of an immense variety of guilds and corporations, as well as students and schoolboys, who filed past the Sultan as he sat viewing the parade from the Imperial Pavilion on the ramparts of the Serai overlooking the street. Such a parade could last for three days or more, during which time all work was suspended. Brilliantly dressed marshals with wands, and seven ceremonial feathers in their head-dresses, called out the commands which signalled the various columns to advance and take their part, while the stewards, imperial pages mounted on agile and manoeuvrable Arab horses, rode up and down through the crowds. The guilds who participated in the procession—on one occasion there were 735—exhibited representations of their craft, sometimes mounted on carts, and as each group passed before the watching Sultan it made a particular effort to interest and divert him. The seamen enacted a mock battle, perhaps between the Sultan's navy and a Cossack boat. Keepers of lunatic asylums led two or three hundred model patients in silver or gilt chains, occasionally dosing them or beating them; an ecclesiastic on a camel read a Koran on a cushion before him, and was surrounded by boys in white, chanting verses. The executioners' guild carried on their display-wagon seventy-seven instruments of torture; the watchmen blew their whistles and pretended to catch thieves in the crowd, causing great commotion. A cart drawn by oxen carried a windmill with boys grinding corn, another carried an oven with boys kneading bread and baking small loaves, and was followed by the pastry-cooks, from whose cart boys threw freshly-made little cakes into the crowd. The furriers' cart was full of realistic stuffed animals; the farmers' was decorated with green boughs and carried reapers with scythes and garlands of corn. The lion-keepers paraded their beasts on ornamental chains, but they kept them in a state of submission by thrusting under their noses lumps of gazelle meat doctored with opium as soon as they showed signs of getting restive. The fishermen's display was not only of harpoons, nets and baskets: before the procession they caught dolphins, sea lions and other large marine creatures which they exhibited bound with cords. The hammals paraded carrying incredible burdens, and the paper-cutters, who were often dervishes, cut strips of paper into fantastic shapes to be used as decorative edgings and borders, and pieces were distributed to be kept as book-marks and souvenirs. The bath orderlies who served with the army demonstrated

135

(1) The Sweepers

52 Guild processions passing before the Sultan on the occasion of the prince's circumcision feast.

(2) The Taxidermists

the felt hammam-tents heated with portable charcoal stoves, of the kind they put up in the evening after a day's march. Seven thousand beggars, blind, lame, paralysed, epileptic, armless, one-legged, naked, barefoot, blundered past with the sheikh of their guild in the middle, seated on an ass; even more numerous were the schoolboys in paper caps, playing tambourines and dodging about among the crowds. Janissary recruits were given the task of keeping the streets clean with shovels and brooms, and scavengers collected the filth and carried it in baskets to dustbins by the seashore; they paid the police superintendent 1000 gold pieces annually for the right to pick over this rubbish.

There were certain secular seasonal festivities apart from those connected with sowing and harvest. In April, on St George's Day, a Greek holiday which the Turks shared under the impression that it commemorated Hizir, the Turkish patron saint, everybody celebrated the Spring Festival. On this date, it was believed, the flowers opened and the nightingales arrived, and all over the country fair-grounds sprang up with the usual entertainments. At the first picnics of the season spring foods like yoghurt, dolma, helva and cheese were eaten, with round flat loaves of yellow barley-bread. On this day too, water from the holy well at Balikli, by the Silivri gate of Istanbul, was sprinkled over or drunk by any of the sick who could make their way or be carried to the courtyard. The very ill were laid on the ground on blankets and the pious threw them coins. In the waters of the well swam certain black-backed fish, the descendants of those supernatural ancestors who, having been fried, jumped from the pan into the water and continued to live and swim. When any of the famous fish were sighted, those near-by uttered a shout of rejoicing, and a murmur of thanks and praise rose from the crowd in response, while the custodians of the well wandered among them collecting money. In fact, places were as important in many rites as dates, as there was a great taste and talent for detail, so that certain corners of a city, or small town, were particularly associated with the festivities of certain days. In Istanbul, for example, it was generally conceded that the finest lettuce appeared in time for the spring celebrations at Yedi Kule, the Seven Towers, while the best place for cockfights was the courtyard of the Fatih mosque.

Other dates were observed annually for precautionary reasons. For the Christians' 9th March, wherever it fell in the Muslim calendar, the astrologers marked the hour and minute of the passing of the sun into another zodiacal house, and this appeared on the almanacs; the exact moment, when it arrived, was the time to eat a paste of particular spices which was believed to render one safe for a year from the bites of snakes and scorpions.

All the observances of religious and secular holidays, however, punctuated a year in which life was lived mainly in privacy, and almost the only entertainment was the exchange of visits, and family occasions. There was very little public provision for the respectable occupation of leisure. Men might sit in the tea-houses playing chess, draughts or backgammon, or they might go to a hammam. In the cook-shops, open to the street, could be seen the turning spits and simmering pots, and tempting smells wandered out to the passer-by, but meals were got through quickly and there was little lingering in the eating-places. There were some respectable cafés which occasionally had verse readings, poetry competitions and dancing, and the money to pay performers was collected in a half-drum from the assembled company.

Coffee appeared in Turkey in 1543, and soon became so popular that it was disapproved of and prohibited; it was re-allowed in 1591 and forbidden again in 1633 (although the ban was always difficult to enforce and eventually lapsed), less because the government considered the drink itself to be particularly noxious than because coffee-houses were haunts of pleasure, vice, and potential sedition. Opium, laudanum and similar drugs, while disapproved of as harmful in excess, never suffered the same ban. The introduction of tobacco in 1601 was to provide another overwhelmingly popular source of communal enjoyment. It too was at first forbidden, but smoking continued in secret and at last became so widespread that towards the end of his reign Murad IV (1623–40) closed the coffee-houses which were the centre of this vice and reinforced the ban. Smoking, however, continued unabated; soldiers kept their short pipes tucked in sleeves or girdles and were constantly caught and punished for smoking in the privies. Finally, in about 1650 the ban was dropped, and the companionable pleasure of smoking in the cafés was freely enjoyed. The nargilehs which they provided for the customers consisted of a crystal bowl, sometimes extremely ornate and beautiful, an ornamented holder at its neck for the luleh, which was the red clay cup which held the tobacco, and a long flexible tube. Into this tube the smoker put his own mouthpiece, and some of these were very beautiful, made of amber set with precious stones, gold and enamels; in fact many men had very fine and valuable collections of these mouth-

53 Men smoking the nargileh and long pipes

pieces. The tobacco used, tumbeki, was of Persian origin; for smoking, a small quantity of it was rolled in a piece of cloth or thin leather and immersed in water, then lifted out, squeezed and rubbed. The luleh was filled with this tobacco, and then a small piece of glowing charcoal was laid on top of it, and the nargileh, its crystal bottle half filled with cooling water, sometimes with the addition of perfume, was placed on the ground. The smoker sat cross-legged, or half reclined, and as he drew on his mouthpiece the water made a soothing bubbling sound; some nargilehs had more than one tube, so that men could share it. There were also nargilehs in the wealthier private houses, but most men had straight tobacco-pipes, both short and long, and many of these too were very ornate and valuable. There were few charms, however, to compare with a skilfully prepared pipe enjoyed in congenial company.

There were also countless coffee-houses and taverns of evil reputation. The drinking of wine was prohibited in Islam, although in realistic fashion there was a Government Inspector of Wine with an office by the Iron Gate at Galata, and the taverns had many Turkish customers. They were not usually kept by Muslims or found in the Muslim quarters, and in any case were never near a mosque; most of them were in the hands of Greeks, Armenians and Jews and were to be found in the Christian and Jewish quarters. There were many taverns near the ports, frequented by sailors and Janissaries and considered to be places of great debauchery. In the cities the prostitutes were usually members of the minority religious groups, and some were established in the cafés of less good reputation, but other popular places of assignation were the creameries and the laundries.

7

Occupations

Almost every man in Turkey was engaged in some sort of recognised occupation: trade, farming, the learned professions or artisans' work. Even in the wealthiest class there were few who devoted their lives entirely to leisure: most were senior employees of the State, and in addition took an active part in the administration of their estates. The exercise of some skill was considered an honourable duty, to such a degree that every Sultan was obliged to learn a craft. Mehmed I made bow-strings; Mehmed II was a keen gardener; Selim I and Suleyman I were goldsmiths; Selim II made crescents for pilgrims' staffs; Murad III was an arrowsmith; Mehmed III and Ahmed I made spoons and archers' thumb-rings; Mehmed IV was a poet and even wrote his military dispatches in verse. They sometimes gave small examples of their craft as gifts to those attending their courts, and it was generally understood that the recipient of such an honour was to reciprocate immediately with a gift of far greater value; but the participation of monarchs in activities so common to their people was a demonstration of the concept of the nobility of work, as well as of solidarity with the religious and humani-- tarian rôle of the trade guilds which controlled it. The conduct of business, too, was of great importance in the empire, and until the period of decline was a respectable and even honoured occupation in which men of all ranks associated freely. Since in the very structure of the domestic system men never came into contact with each other's families there was no risk of inter-marriage, and consequently class, ethnic and religious distinctions were no barrier to satisfactory and remunerative trade connections, and to easy relations between, for example, educated men of affairs, able but unlettered merchants, infidel shipping agents and simple craftsmen.

Considerable state supervision was exercised, and all sales and pur- chases, particularly those involving import or export, were covered by some regulation. The captains of all trading vessels were required to produce a licence from the Turkish government, as were any merchant, his agents and his staff, who needed additional authentication to cover any branches of his business which he might have in other towns. Both Turkish and European employers had to notify the government when an employee left their service and his papers had to be surrendered; new documents had to be taken out for new employees. No goods were allowed to be sold to foreigners either inside or outside the country without the general authorisation and the particular permission of the relevant government department. Exports were rigidly controlled, and consisted only of surpluses which were certain not to be needed. With rare exceptions food was never sold abroad, neither was wood that might be used for shipbuilding, nor minerals. The principal exports were leather, skins and wools and, to a lesser extent, wax, cotton, silk, linen, alum, certain woods and spices, and, more rarely still, caviare, pearls and porcelain.

In internal commerce the needs of the government came first, those of artisans second and private individuals last. The principal industries of the empire were primarily concerned with the production of war materials, and while they had first call on all raw materials they also accounted for a great deal of prosperity: at Samakar alone, a small town south of Sofia, there were seventeen iron factories engaged in the making of spades, anchors, horseshoes, nails and similar products for the armed forces. A large part of the textile industry was engaged in making tent-cloths, ropes and sails in addition to cloth for uniforms; work in fur and skins, which included saddle-and shoe-making, was also largely for military purposes. The main imports were fabrics, paper, sugarloaf and spices from the east, glass, silk, mirrors and drugs from Europe and particularly Venice, tin, iron and lead from England; but the empire was so huge and provided such a variety of goods that there was very little need to import anything except luxuries, and the army and navy were largely supplied by native products.

Official responsibility was not limited to paper-work. At Tophane was situated the great gun foundry at which the heavy artillery of the imperial army was made. On the day when a cannon was to be cast the Grand Master of Artillery, the Chief Overseer, the Imam and the Muezzin attached to the foundry, and the Time Keeper, Master, foreman and founders assembled. To the accompaniment of invocations of the name of God, logs of wood were thrown into the furnace to begin the process. Twenty-four hours later the ironfounders and the stokers stripped until they were wearing nothing but slippers, a cap pulled down over the head, leaving the eyes visible, and a pair of thick sleeves; in addition, forty sheikhs and viziers, including the Grand Vizier and the Sheikh-ul-Islam, were admitted. All others were excluded for fear of the Evil Eye. Throughout the ensuing performance the viziers and sheikhs repeated unceasingly 'There is no power and strength save in

God'. As they intoned this the master craftsmen threw hundredweights of tin into the cauldrons of molten brass. At a crucial moment the head founder called on the viziers and sheikhs to throw some coins into the brazen sea as alms 'in the name of the True Faith', and stirred the gold and silver into the metal with long poles. When the brass began to bubble it was a sign that the metals were fused; more wood was thrown into the furnaces and the most dangerous moment of all approached. The company rose to its feet and the Time Keeper gave the warning that in half an hour the mouth of the furnace was to be opened. Prayers for the success of this were offered with fervent devotion, and when the half hour expired, on a signal from the Time Keeper and to the repetition of 'Allah, Allah' the head founder and the master workmen opened the furnace door with iron hooks, and the glowing, burning metal gushed out into the channels which led to the moulds. At this moment the viziers and sheikhs, who had put on white shirts, sacrificed on either side of the furnace the forty or fifty sheep which had been brought in. It took half an hour to fill the largest mould, which was made from clay from the little village of Sariyer on the Bosphorus. When the mould was filled the stream of brass was stopped by a mass of oily clay and diverted to flow into the next mould, to the accompaniment of fresh prayers. If the casting were successfully concluded, with none of the terrible accidents that so often marred this operation, prayers of thanks were said, pay increases granted, seventy robes of honour distributed, and all shared a celebratory feast.

In the case of artisans engaged on general trade, the needs of those working in Istanbul were supplied before those of the provinces, and all were under government control. Workmen who needed a particular material for the pursuance of their trade, for example the cauldron-makers of Sivas, Tokat and Amasya who bought copper from the mines at Kastamonu, had to have a document of authorisation bearing the official seal for their transactions. But, in spite of the bureaucratic machine, trade flourished, and the supervision was often benign: in the major industry of metallurgy the government strictly controlled the genuineness and purity of silver and gold, and also protected the interests of artisans in these metals by allowing them to handle the distribution and sale of lower-priced European goods.

The production of food was a source of employment throughout the country. As a result, food was cheap, particularly in the cities, and plentiful: the produce of some regions was assigned in its entirety to Istanbul. The catching and preserving of fish was a considerable in-dustry. Many fishermen favoured angling with deep sea lines made of horsehair, each with two or three baited hooks and with a plummet and cork. To catch crabs, lobsters and smaller fish, twenty or more bell-shaped wicker pots were tied together with strong cord, weighted with a stone

54 *Nets rigged for mullet-fishing by night. In the foreground a body is being disposed
of after execution*

and sunk, the place marked with a buoy made of a couple of empty
gourds which floated on the water. Sometimes teams of six boats were
arranged in a rectangle about 40 yards by 25, with nets of strong tanned
twine slung between them; these were placed in the passage of migratory
fish, and made enormous catches. By another method, stationary nets
were submerged and watched by men perched high on lookouts; when
a shoal swam over they signalled to the fishermen waiting in flat-
bottomed craft, who hastily raised the nets and pulled them in. Many of
the sturdy curved-prow fishing boats sailed at night with bright flares
hung over the side to attract the fish, and when the men had made their
catch they rowed up and down shouting and chaffering with the invisible
wholesalers on the shore until a price was agreed upon, before they
would come alongside to deliver their cargo. During a ten-week season
beginning in the autumn, swordfish, tunny and mackerel, which had
come from the cold waters of the Black Sea to lay their eggs, were caught
by these flare-boats in shoals as they passed through the Bosphorus. The
fish markets were always the filthiest corners of the city, with steep slimy
streets and tumbled baskets of stinking garbage. Some of the smaller fish,
like mackerel, were slit open and dried on racks in the sun; others were
cut up and salted for the winter, and the shells of mussels were split to
provide mother-of-pearl for lower-grade inlay work on the many objects
of carved wood in daily use.

Thousands of men were employed on construction work in all its branches. Skilled workmen such as carpenters and stone-cutters earned twice as much as unskilled labourers, and everybody's daily rate of pay was lower in winter, that is, from the beginning of November until the beginning of May, because the days were shorter.

The list of occupations, in fact, is almost endless, and provided employment for all who needed it, but there was little mobility because of the restrictions imposed by the guilds. Throughout Ottoman Turkey, a man's allegiances were, in order of priority, to his guild, to his religion and to the Sultan, that is, the State, and it is impossible to over-estimate the importance in the social structure of the rôle of the guilds. Their authority was unassailable; they were autonomous, and since most towns and villages were economically self-contained the semi-independent guild units remained comparatively unaffected by the political vicissitudes of the empire. They had their origin in a chivalric brotherhood, the Ahis, of righteous unmarried men who chose their leader and gave him all they earned, out of which money the cost of food and other expenses of the group were met. By Ottoman times only the tanners, saddlers, leather workers and shoemakers remained as members of the Ahi brotherhood; for most it had lost its quasi-religious form and become a series of trade unions individual to each craft.

By the beginning of the sixteenth century a body of laws had grown up governing the place and tools of work of guild members, and all trades, professions and businesses were exercised under concessions and monopolies. A specified number of craftsmen were authorised to practise in each trade within a fixed area, and the number of shops and businesses permitted to operate there was also regulated. Two kinds of warrant, or gedik, could be issued to craftsmen: one gave an individual the right to practise wherever he liked, but the other was valid only for a man exercising his craft in a specific location, a particular shop or booth; if an artisan wanted to ensure long and undisputed possession of his place of trade he asked his guild to register his tools and goods in this category, and was given a certificate to guarantee his rights. If a craftsman wanted to transfer his rights in his premises to another, even his son, he needed permission, and if he wanted to move to another town, or even street, he had to renew his patent. The state was initially opposed to these restrictions, but the guilds insisted and had their way, claiming the right to protect their members. In this spirit of paternalism, the upper prices of goods were periodically fixed; also, when a trade prospered, more gediks were granted, and when the popularity of its products waned warrants were allowed to lapse and the number of craftsmen operating thus decreased, so that there was never either the stimulus or the anxiety of competition. But the scope of each guild was strictly limited: innovations of any kind were strongly disapproved of, and no changes of fashion permitted. The guilds brought order, discipline, good standards of workmanship and such a strong sense of professional solidarity that shopkeepers who had made their first sale of the day would often pass the next prospective purchaser on to one who had not; but routine procedures, monopoly of production, absence of rivalry and the discouragement of inventiveness sometimes brought in their wake considerable artistic stagnation.

Each guild was composed of masters, journeymen or master-apprentices, and ordinary apprentices, organised in a rigid hierarchy under its sheikh, with a steward and disciplinary officer responsible for its honour. Although village craftsmen were also guild members the organisation was predominantly urban, and loyalties were local rather than national: even government recognition of guild claims was brought about by pressure from lodges in Istanbul on accessible ministers in the capital. Each guild had a room, a lonja, in the town, where affairs were discussed and disputes among members settled. The elders sat on a raised platform, the others present on the floor; any below the rank of master were not admitted. Although some disciplinary matters were referred to the cadi, as many as possible were arbitrated within the guild, and the steward charged with the duty of meting out the punishment decided on by the elders had a whip and cane which were hung on the wall for all to see. Craftsmen found guilty of offences in which the honour of the guild was brought into disrepute were suspended or, in extreme cases, expelled altogether, and so effectively deprived of the means of making a decent living. The governing body met on the first and third Fridays of each month, when members were expected to report anything they had seen or heard which might affect their interests; there were also reports from the two members who had been charged with investigating the circumstances of those requesting a loan from the guild chest. This was a common assistance fund to which all members made weekly or monthly contributions, and which was used partly for religious purposes, for example annual Koran readings at the mosque in Ramadan and distribution of food to the poor, and partly for the needs of any guild members who had fallen ill or were in financial distress. It paid funeral expenses if the family had no money, and it made loans at an interest rate of 1% to master-craftsmen who wanted to extend their businesses. Men also contributed to, and could draw on, the community chest of their quarter, which was fed by donations from the local inhabitants, by money promised when a wish was made and given when it was fulfilled, or by gifts made with superstitious reverence at the start of some enterprise. This money could be borrowed by the needy at a very low rate of interest, and was used for such domestic necessities as the rebuilding of burned houses, or assistance to orphans.

Every apprentice was attached to a master who taught him the mysteries of his craft and the traditions of the guild, and vouched for him when he was qualified. The years of training were long and exacting, and when at last the youth might be considered fit for initiation his father would consult the sheikh who, if he agreed that the candidate was indeed ready, invited the masters of the trade to meet for the ceremony at the guild room; occasionally the ceremony took place at the father's house if it were big enough or, if several lads were ready for admission, at an open-air picnic party. The apprentice prepared several examples of his work which he submitted to be examined by a council of craftsmen, and if passed they were displayed on a silver tray on the day of his admittance. After the recital of a ceremonial prayer the boy's master presented his apprentice, who kneeled in front of the sheikh and kissed his hand. The sheikh put his hand on the boy's shoulder and adjured him to keep the faith and observe the regulations of his guild. The master then gave a towel to the sheikh, who tied it round the boy's waist, like an apron, and then whispered certain arcane secrets of the craft and guild into his ear, thereby initiating him into full membership, an adult and honourable status. The newly-made master, as he now was, kissed the hands of every guildsman present, and was congratulated by those whose equal he could now proudly claim to be. To the beating of drums and the playing of fifes the disciplinary officer declaimed a welcome on behalf of the whole trade, and then proceeded to sell by auction the objects which the former apprentice had made. These were always bought by those present at far more than they were worth, and the money was given to the new master as capital with which to set up his own shop. For father, master and son it was a day of tremendous pride and solemnity; the rights and duties of guild membership affected all aspects of a man's public life, and were with him to the end of his days.

Every now and then, perhaps at intervals of between ten and twenty years, there was a large joint guild festivity in some open place: it was usually the opportunity for a huge picnic excursion into the countryside. These were both social reunions and exhibitions of work, with booths demonstrating aspects of the various crafts, and some of the finest examples of workmanship were offered to the Sultan, particularly if the festivity coincided with an occasion of official rejoicing. Sometimes the Sultan reciprocated with a gift of silver or gold plate, which the guild used on ceremonial occasions in addition to the valuable plate and utensils which it had bought for the honour of the lonja, and which were held in common. The cost of such purchases, and the expenses of festivities and parties, were defrayed from levies on members and not drawn from the guild chest.

The government exercised as much supervision as possible over the guilds, partly as a means of controlling the working population, and partly to protect the workers themselves and to reinforce the aims and standards of their own governing bodies: it assisted in preventing un-employment by refusing to allow the importation of competing wares, it controlled rents, it permitted new workshops to be opened only when the demand justified it. But each town in the empire big enough to have a cadi, had an inspector who was concerned exclusively with the affairs of guilds and the collection of the various dues on their goods and transactions; he also collected money from them for his own and his staff's salaries. These inspectors had the right of summary punishment. They kept a register listing all the guilds in the town and the artisans in each, as well as the kind and quantity of goods kept in the shops. If unsatisfactory work was reported to them, or if as a result of market inspection they found that goods were badly or wrongly made, they seized and destroyed them, and the offending shops might be temporarily or permanently closed as a punishment. For lesser infringements a tradesman could be bastinadoed in front of his shop; for more serious offences the penalty was imprisonment, with or without hard labour, for a minimum of two or three months and possibly indefinitely. Guild elders could appeal to the cadi for redress against the inspectors, but these were seldom irresponsible. Certain of the very old organisations, such as the tanners and saddlers, the Egyptian spice market of Istanbul, the silk market and the street of linen weavers, had exacted from Mehmed the Conqueror an order forbidding the police inspectors to enter their precincts, and they were proud of their immunity. Also, in the reign of Suleyman the Magnificent, in spite of the ban on Janissaries indulging in trade some of them began to infiltrate into the markets, and while many contented themselves with extorting money from shopkeepers others actually set up in business; these ignored tax demands and avoided punishment from market inspectors by claiming their right to be tried by their own officers and sentenced, if at all, to a Janissary prison. But fear of the law as well as pride in their craft meant that on the whole there was a high degree of honesty among guild members.

Not all guilds were artisanal: there were also organisations of the intellectual and scientific members of the liberal professions, which included men of religion, poets and chroniclers, public scribes and petition-writers as well as bookbinders, paper- and ink-sellers and men who kept bookshops. These were all Muslim guilds as were the druggists, the house-painters and certain others. Until 1768 guilds generally had members of any religion; in that year separate organisations were set up for Jews and Christians, but some trades had always been exclusively Muslim including 90% of those involving foodstuffs. The doctors, surgeons and oculists were frequently members of the minorities, and even foreigners; there were many Jews among them. Another category of non-craftsmen were the entertainers, and there were seventy-one musicians' guilds alone, not counting those that made musical instruments. They included the mehter, who were the official bandsmen in the service of the Sultan and of some administrators of high rank, as well as the musicians who performed at guild and dervish ceremonies and for private parties, and those who played the accompaniment to dancers or reciters, or for theatrical performances. The guilds of beggars, prostitutes, pick-pockets and thieves, who paid their taxes to the police and observed faithfully the discipline of their organisations, were among the oldest established and dated from well before Ottoman times. The guild of thieves also acted as a kind of clearing-house for 'lost' property: when a man had been robbed he made representations to their sheikh, offering a sum of money for the safe return of his valuables. If the price was fair and the thieves had nothing against the man, his property was enquired for, collected, and returned to him. In the category of miscellaneous workmen were the bath attendants, water-carriers, gardeners, boatmen and low-grade municipal employees; in yet another group were the pedlars and itinerant salesmen.

All the guilds were closely linked with one or other of the sects and usually subscribed to a religious order; the title of sheikh given to the head of their organisations was a religious one, and religious ceremonies formed part of the initiation process. There were always mosques near the places of work, some actually subject to certain guilds. Each guild had one or two patron saints, usually a Hebrew patriarch who was credited with being the inventor of the craft or trade, or a Companion of the Prophet or even the Prophet himself, and each shopkeeper had hanging in his booth a little verse including the name of his saint. Seth was considered to be the patron of weavers, Noah of merchants and sailors, Abraham of dairymen, David of armourers and blacksmiths, Ishmael of hunters, Joseph of clock-makers, Jonah of fishermen, Jesus of travellers, Lot of chroniclers, Ezra of vintners, Adam of sowers, Moses of shepherds, Anas ibn Malik of police officers and Zulnoon the Egyptian of doctors; Muhammad himself was the patron saint of merchants, poets, story-tellers, clerks and many others.

The guilds of the eastern provinces of the empire were similar in construction, with perhaps even stronger demonstrations of religious affiliation both at the initiation ceremonies and in public manifestations. The quality of workmanship was somewhat lower. There were in the east some few very fine craft secrets, jealously guarded by a handful of families who would not even share them within the guild, but these families either eventually died out, or, because of the constant demand for excellence on the part of the Sultan and the court, were transplanted to Istanbul or other big Turkish cities.

Because of strong guild affiliation, the expression of most forms of art in Turkey was influenced by a comparative constancy of taste and the

55 Seljuk mausoleum   *56 Doorway of the Seljuk Injeminare medrese in Konya*

requirement of a high standard of workmanship, rather than by fluctuations in style and the periodic inspiration of genius.

The Turkish heritage included a number of beautiful objects and sites left from the classical period in Asia Minor. Although racked by earthquakes, ravaged for building-stone and pillaged of superb columns for incorporation into mosques, enough remained standing or was turned up by the plough to present some image of antique beauty. Representation of the human or animal form was forbidden in Islam, and a number of classical figures were destroyed as the work of godless idolators, but many retained enough majesty or magic to be preserved as miracle-working objects of popular worship, and so became part of the daily scene. A good deal remained of the monuments of the Seljuk Empire which had preceded the Ottomans. The great artistic flowering in the thirteenth century had produced splendid mosques, medreses and khans many of which continued in use throughout the Ottoman period. Their typical and ubiquitous mausolea, although not copied, were much admired. They consisted of a round or octagonal chamber over a square base, containing the cenotaph, with the tomb in the crypt below and a conical roof over all, and they were built of stone with geometric, floral and even animal designs, in artistic defiance of the restrictions of Islam. The Seljuk mosques were decorated mainly on the façade and about the mihrab with similar carvings in high relief. The vast khans were built a day's journey apart, a distance of between 20 and 25 miles, on the main highways. They were complex and highly developed units, but composed basically of a court with rooms on three sides and a large and very solid longitudinal hall with a high central nave and a number of lower aisles opening off it at right angles; the centre dome rested on a high drum. They were usually well fortified, with massive walls and slit windows; mosque, rooms and stabling provided all facilities, and the whole combined fitness for its purpose with perfection of proportion.

The wood-carving of the Seljuks was also very fine, and much of it remained on the doors of mosques and other buildings, and on the pulpits and Koran-stands. They also made superb bronze holders for mosque oil lamps, pierced in openwork design and suspended on immense chains. The prayer carpets of the period were sober, and limited in colour almost entirely to blues, reds and greens. The ceramic arts were highly developed, although here too there was little variety of colour: principally turquoise, lapis lazuli, black and brown. Much use was made of blue tiles on the exterior of buildings, and the fluted-roofed mausoleum of the founder of the sect of whirling dervishes, at Konya, was a remarkable example. The decorative work was much esteemed: panels of old Seljuk tiles with geometric patterns, and flowers, and stylised human or animal figures were carefully cut out of crumbling old buildings and set in the walls of palace rooms.

57   Wooden Koran-stand – Seljuk

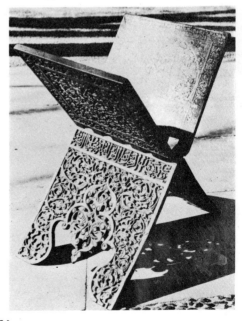

During the Turkish migrations many artists and craftsmen had settled in neighbouring eastern countries and carried their art-forms to Persia, Iraq, Egypt and Syria; they rebuilt Konya and founded many new cities. In return craftsmen came from Damascus, Aleppo, Samarkand and many other centres, each place contributing its specialities of form and method. In the golden age of Suleyman especially, craftsmen and workers in all fields including poets, writers and historians of skill were assembled to enjoy the patronage of the Sultan and the many wealthy Viziers and civil servants, and to assist in the

58 The Selimiye mosque at Edirne, which the architect Sinan considered his greatest work

glorification of Istanbul. On the other hand, the strong traditional element and purity of workmanship in Turkey was much admired abroad, and Suleyman's architect Sinan sent his skilled pupils to construct monuments for Agra, in India, at the request of that city. Indeed, architecture was the richest and most flourishing branch of Ottoman art. Although their marvellous mosques may have been inspired originally by the church of St. Sophia which fell into Ottoman hands at the conquest of the city, they underwent enormous development. The great Sinan began his career as a building worker; during his subsequent service in the army, his skill began to emerge and he was commissioned to design and build bridges and barracks and arsenals. From military assignments he progressed to the construction of religious buildings, until finally he was summoned to Istanbul by Suleyman the Magnificent, and built the greatest mosque complexes the country was ever to hold. His feeling for proportion and the balance of mass, minarets and domes was as superbly true as his supervision of detail was thorough, and his work was the inspiration of mosque building everywhere. The fever of building which he initiated did not stop until the seventeenth century, and his style and standards remained the touchstone, yet he thought not as an artist but as a mastercraftsman. He himself said: 'Shehzade mosque was my apprenticeship, the Suleymaniye my journeyman's work, the Selimiye at Edirne my masterpiece.'

The decoration of buildings flourished accordingly. Ceilings were highly ornamented, carved and painted, coffered, gilded. The interiors of mosque domes were bright with fresh colour in symmetrical and perfectly-spaced designs; private houses might have silver stars set in a blue sky. Cupboards and panelling were equally finely worked. The ceramic art which had produced the blue tiles of Konya in the thirteenth century, and the delicate Persian workmanship of the fourteenth and fifteenth, was revived as ceramicists were brought from Tabriz in Persia to found workshops in Iznik and Istanbul. Following the old style they

59   Tiled panels with

(1) calligraphy   (2) plum blossom and flowers

60 Portrait of Selim II (1566–74)

made panels of flowers and trees which lined palace rooms and decorated the walls of mosques and rich houses. Other craftsmen brought patterns distinctive to their place of origin: calligraphy from Jerusalem, cypresses and fruit-blossom from Damascus, and a variety of others. Elements of Chinese conventions were assimilated and incorporated: the famous cloud-pattern, transformed sometimes into floating ribbons, began to appear on fabrics as well as tiles. They painted and stencilled realistic and precise flowers, especially the favourite tulips and carnations as well as roses, hyacinths, and leaves and palmettes in continuous designs, meticulously matching from tile to tile. To the range of colours they added purple, yellow and green, and a brilliant white for background and calligraphy. The pottery at Iznik made tiles for the restoration of the Dome of the Rock in Jerusalem, one of the oldest shrines in Islam, and they produced for the first time anywhere a really reliable brilliant scarlet which was so thick and rich that it stood out on the tile in relief. The ceramicists and their glass-worker colleagues also made beautiful mosque lamps, sometimes decorated with a flowing calligraphic design, as well as vases, sherbet-bottles, water-pipe bowls and a variety of decorated utensils.

In spite of the prejudice against the depicting of human and animal figures, they occurred in all branches of the pictorial arts. Persian and Moghul artists portrayed mythological, religious and historical subjects in large frescoes as well as portraits and miniatures, but in Turkey, in order not to offend popular sentiment, these were more strictly kept from the public although Sultans and connoisseurs possessed them for their private enjoyment. Most of the Sultans also relaxed the rules far enough to have their portraits painted, brightly coloured and in static and decorative poses, but with individual, realistic, and even unflattering detail of feature. The art of miniature painting reached its peak in the sixteenth century. The fastidious and exquisite medium of these stories-

in-pictures of kings and victories may have had its origin in the art of
gilding, from which developed an intermediate stage of illuminating; certainly the artist possessed many skills. Manuscript illustrations followed

*61 Procession passing before the Sultan's guests. In the bottom balcony near the door
are members of Frankish embassies. From the Surnameh of Murad III, 16th century*

62   Illuminated manuscript

the inspiration of Persian miniaturists but demonstrated a distinctive Turkish style, with simpler figures, architecture and landscape, and greater spatial clarity. Whereas the Persian motif was usually a hero or a romantic aspect of the nation's remote past, Turkish artists were concerned with contemporary or recent achievements of the house of Osman. They followed the basic Persian conventions of a high vantage point, the main scene set in the middle-ground against architecture or landscape, and flat puppet-like figures, but included great detail of garments, arms and uniform. One of the finest illustrated manuscripts was the Surnameh, which recorded in pictures the 40-day-long circumcision feast, in 1583, of the son of Sultan Murad III. In each scene the same audience, consisting of the Sultan and his company, sat in the background, occasionally changing their pose and gesture; in the foreground passed before them, vigorous and lifelike, the displays of the craft guilds.

Books were made of beautifully hand-written pages, seldom sewn together, placed in folded fascicules of ten sheets in a leather-covered case which was tinted, gilded and embossed or inlaid. The manuscripts themselves, with occasional illuminations, were written with reed pens along lines of only faintly visible indentations, made by pressing the paper onto a card across which even rows of string had been stretched and glued. The Korans and their commentaries were, of course, of particularly magnificent workmanship. As for the content of non-religious books, the formality of education and the strong traditionalism of form exercised some limitation on intellectual exercise, even in the realms of literature and sometimes under quite enlightened patronage. The high-flown language in which much of it was written was unintelligible to all but the most highly educated Turks, consisting as it did mainly of Arabic and Persian words. Of poetry, the most admired form was the gazel, of from five to fifteen lines formally constructed and romantically turned; many of these were learned by heart in youth, and declaimed at nostalgic and sentimental moments at parties in later life. Equally formal in verse and rhyme arrangement were the epic poems and elegiacs. Many masters of poetry and literature—Fuzuli of Baghdad, Baki,

63 Calligraphy in the form of a caique

Revani, Hayali, Nefi and Yahya—wrote in the sixteenth century, and cultural taste remained faithful to them. Another literary form was official historiography, and foremost in this field were the writings of Naima, who died in 1716. Geographical works included map-making, nautical astronomy, travel accounts and descriptions of foreign lands and seas. Evliya Chelebi wrote ten volumes of travel books, frequently undependable as he drew freely on his imagination, but expressed, exceptionally, in simple language. There was a considerable body of religious literature written in the popular language, mainly the lives of the saints, mystical or magical tales and dervish stories, in addition to non-religious legends in narrative poetry, and verses on such themes as love and beauty. But the myths and stories that entertained the greater number of the people were in the custody of the public story-tellers, committed to memory and passed on down the generations. A form of literary invention which required great ingenuity was the composition of chronograms, which appeared on tombs and fountains, as a heading to poems and elsewhere. They depended on the convention of a numerical value for each letter, and took the form of a neatly-turned phrase or verse the letters of which added up to a number, which was the date which the monument commemorated.

Carpet-making, originally a folk craft, became a highly-developed skill of great technical artistry. There had been for many years a persistence of fairly fixed patterns, basically simple, with bold character and strong colours, and with a rather coarse weave and hard knot. Then, as greater cultural interchange began to take place between cities, hastened by the Ottoman expansion into Azerbaijan and Egypt, new artistic principles, colours and techniques were adopted by the Turkish weavers. The red vegetable dye from Persia which was to give Turkish carpets their characteristic colour became an exclusive and closely-guarded secret, and the typical Persian carpet motif, of a central medallion with quarter-medallions in the corners, was added to their repertoire of styles,

64 *Prayer-rug from Gordes*

but it was the combination of the Persian knot, the silky Egyptian wool with its subtle dyes, and modifications of the traditional Turkish patterns that made up one of the finest manifestations of Ottoman art. Whether silk or wool was used for the warp and weft, the new knot was always tied in wool or cotton, which brought the ends of the pile close together and so produced an effect of fine velvet. The patterns included curved, veined leaves, rosettes, tendrils and naturalistic blossoms; the design of prayer-rugs was built up around a clear niche-shaped space woven of one colour. In all rugs there was a tiny deliberate mistake, perhaps one or two knots of white intruding into the ground of another colour, to avoid the envy of the Evil Eye which was bound to fall on any object of perfection.

Fabrics were expertly woven, whether transparent muslins or heavy gold-thread brocades. Most were extremely rich, and some designs had been made continuously since Seljuk times; highly esteemed among these was a cloth of silk and flax, with flowers in cut velvet relief. Some textile mills wove exclusively on wide looms, and specialised in certain designs and colours so as to produce fabric particularly suited for divan covers, while others made narrower rolls for cushions, garments and a myriad other purposes. The greatest silk centre was Bursa, but subsequently Istanbul and many other cities began to weave in response to the tremendous demand, and at one time the entire population of Amasya was occupied with some aspect or other of silk production. Fine embroidery, with coloured silks and gold and silver thread, was both a domestic and professional art, and appeared on towels, slippers, kerchiefs and garments.

Although the making of jewellery included much delicate workmanship, a Turkish speciality in coarser taste consisted in setting precious and semi-precious stones, frequently uncut, in almost everything that could

158

be decorated, including even porcelain cups and the binding of books. Thrones were usually superb examples of the art of goldsmith and jeweller: in form a large square seat, usually with a canopy and a large jewelled ornament mounted in gold suspended overhead, they were made, to the taste of the reigning Sultan, of rare woods or precious metals, inlaid with pearls and gems of unimaginable richness.

Of the performing arts, music had the widest and perhaps most class-less appeal. The Sultan's entourage included singers and instrumental-ists whose speciality was the presentation of classical music, as well as the mehter, the army band. For classical music and accompaniment to song and dance the principal musical instruments were the kemancheh, the kanun, the lute and the ney, or flute; for weddings, processions and certain dances there was in addition a variety of drums of all sizes, from the huge tinned copper kettle-drums to the darbuka, an hourglass-shaped earthenware pot with sheep- or goat-skin across one or both ends. The kemancheh was a kind of violin with a hemispherical sounding body, originally a half-coconut with fish-skin stretched across it, and a long neck. A common variety had two strings each made up of about sixty horsehairs, and was played with a yard-long bow of ash-wood and horsehair. It had an iron foot, on which it was pivoted from side to side while being played. The kanun was a variety of dulcimer of orna-mented wood, usually walnut, and played with two plectra worn on the fore-finger of each hand. The lute had seven double strings, two to a note, of lamb's gut, which were plucked with a plectrum made for preference of a slip of vulture's feather. There were many kinds and sizes of flute made of reed or cane; tambourines and minor stringed instruments, like inferior fiddles, were also common, as were such clicking instruments as casta-nets, spoons and sticks. Group singing was much enjoyed, especially during picnic and boating parties, and this was frequently followed by solo per-

65 Caftan of silk and velvet, woven in the stylized design derived from the Chinese cloud motif

66 Instrumentalists of the army band

formances which were freely interrupted by admiring interjections from the crowd.

The mehter, or army bands, were allotted to certain officials, whose rank dictated their size. The imperial mehter, which began each day's duties by playing to wake the inhabitants of the Palace for the dawn prayer, was composed of ninety musicians. The mehter of the Grand Vizier had forty-five, that of the Chief Admiral had thirty, as did a provincial governor's. They performed on ceremonial occasions, daily following the afternoon prayer, and after the noon prayers on Fridays and holy days. These sessions lasted twenty minutes, during which the audience remained standing, since these were in fact religious exercises, a form of prayer for the Sultan, called gulbenk. The instruments were varieties of fifes and drums, cymbals and tambourines, and the performance concluded with all the musicians bowing deeply and intoning a long-drawn-out 'Hu-u-u-u-u'; there was a distinctive war-time gulbenk to arouse the zeal of the soldiers. An army band also played for the Janissaries, who recited: 'Kerim Allah, rahim Allah'—'Bountiful God, merciful God'—as they marched. Their spectacular ceremonial step was performed to the beat of one-two-three-pause; that is, left, right, left, then a rest for the fourth beat with the back foot held in position slightly raised, then a right, left, right, rest, and so on. On the day of the pilgrim caravan's departure for Mecca the Janissary mehter played in the streets, wandering from quarter to quarter collecting money, and it was they who brought tidings of appointments to high office by playing outside the house of the fortunate man.

Much loved, and practised with artistry and skill, was the occupation of gardening. The roses, carnations, hyacinths, tulips and fruit-blossom which were reproduced on tiles, carvings, fountains and fabrics were cultivated with devotion, and the summer kiosks of the noble families were set among perfectly-kept formal arrangements of blossoming plants that glowed like carpets. In the seventeenth century the passion for tulips led some collectors and cultivators of the bulb into extravagances that ended in financial ruin. The period from 1703 to 1730 was known in Turkish history as the Age of Tulips, when evening parties were given in the gardens, during which tortoises with small oil lamps on their backs crept among the beds of flowers.

8

Life in Anatolia

The territories of the Ottoman Empire fell, more or less, into four categories. In the first were those most directly administered, according to a complicated but fairly uniform pattern, and comprising Rumelia and Anatolia and some of the nearer provinces. Then came certain regions governed under special regulations, such as Egypt and the holy cities of Mecca and Medina. In a third category were some provinces, such as Rumania and Transylvania, which maintained a certain control over their administration, in consideration of the payment of tribute. A fourth group were the protected or vassal states which were very loosely attached and paid no tribute, like parts of Arabia, and Crim Tartary, a state whose royal house, it was generally understood, was heir to the throne of Turkey if the Ottoman line should ever die out. Apart from the lands which acknowledged the suzerainty of the Sultan while retaining a large degree of control over their own affairs, the greater part of the empire was divided into areas, each administered by a governor who was appointed for a term of office by the central government. Numbers of these were grouped together under a Governor-General, each entitled to bear a sanjak, or standard, composed of a lance with a gold-plated brass ball on the top and a number of horse-tails—originally yak-tails—depending from it. They were the symbols of royalty and vice-royalty, and the number of horse-tails indicated the importance of the holder, thus, a governor was entitled to one, a Governor-General to two, the Grand Vizier to five and the Sultan himself paraded with as many as nine.

67 Head of a standard of three horse-tails

Each governor was to his province what the Sultan was to the empire: in peacetime he was the civil authority, and in time of war the provincial troops rallied to his standard, and it was this

162

68 Provincial town house. The harem quarters in the middle of the upper floor have close-shuttered windows

combination of civil and military functions that defined his position as vice-regal. It was the pride of each governor to make his headquarters a microcosm of palace life, and to recreate for himself, even in the furthest corners of the empire, the civilised way of life of Istanbul. Town life in Anatolia was not so great an exile to members of the administration as that in some provinces. Those princes of the imperial house who were undergoing their training were never sent to governorates in Rumelia: they would be too close to the standing armies which they might suborn and start an insurrection. They were therefore seconded to Anatolia, and as a result a number of fine provincial palaces were established in some of the larger towns, which became centres of considerable architectural and cultural activity. Life in the Anatolian countryside, however, preserved intact for hundreds of years the features of primitive simplicity imposed by feudal restrictions and geographical inaccessibility. Because of the distinguishing standard, the territorial divisions themselves came to be known as sanjaks; each sanjak was sub-divided into a number of smaller regions, some urban and some rural, centred on villages. To each region was appointed a cadi to apply Muslim law and an army officer who represented the administration, but except for the demands of the tax collector the real arbiter of village life was the local mufti, a title sometimes awarded honorifically to the wise man, whose claims to religious learning might be small indeed.

Rural taxation was not applied uniformly throughout the empire. Rumelia and Anatolia were treated differently in this context from the eastern dominions, and were taxed generally to the amount of between 10% and 20% of the yield of the land, sometimes in cash and sometimes in kind. The taxation of Muslims took the form of tithes; non-Muslims, on the other hand, paid a poll tax on adult males in addition to an income tax and a tax on production similar to the tithes, and only ministers of religion of these minority peoples were exempt. There were in addition a number of arbitrary taxes which included customs dues, patent fees, judicial costs, taxes on marriage and on bachelors, and a variety of fines, all variable according to the requirements or greed of the Sultan and his subordinates. They were applied both to Muslim and non-Muslim, although generally not at the same rate: when, for example, the customs dues paid by Muslims was 4%, the minorities paid 5%, and Europeans resident in Turkey paid, under the Capitulations, only 3%. In 1481, after the reign of Mehmed the Conqueror, the collecting of taxes was farmed out to the highest bidders, who undertook to ensure that the government received the sum it had asked for and, incidentally, made a handsome profit for themselves by extorting even more, under a variety of pretexts. This tax-collecting concession was at first granted for one year, but after Mustafa II (1695–1703) it was awarded for life, and eventually even became hereditary; in this way it never fell into the hands of infidels. The system protected the Treasuries from the defections of weak or venal tax collectors, but it exposed the people to unfair and even tyrannical demands. There were two Treasuries, one enriched by taxes and tribute from the public, and the other the Sultan's own. This consisted originally of one-fifth of all booty and especially of prisoners of war; to this were added the revenues from Egypt and Arabia, a 10% death duty from all subjects, the property which he inherited automatically on the death of slave civil servants, and of course the rich presents which he constantly received.

The Sultan owned all land in Anatolia which was not endowed for the purpose of waqf, and except with his consent, or that of his representative, no change of tenure was possible.

In Turkish cosmology the earth was flat and surrounded by an ocean, which was in turn encircled by a chain of mountains; this was the uppermost of seven earths, while overhead, one above the other, stretched seven heavens. Their knowledge of immediate geographical features was, however, more practical. Their many military campaigns, and the reports of governors and tax assessors, as well as those of pilgrims and traders, combined with their specialists' surveys to provide a detailed body of information on the disposition of mountain ranges and plains, woodland and rivers, mining and cultivable areas. The regulations governing land tenure and exploitation of natural resources in Anatolia were precisely defined, and admitted of nine categories. Some areas were arid or marshy, unsuitable for cultivation; others were defined as either urban or village, and included gardens and vegetable plots; pasture land supported the main Anatolian occupation of rearing animals for hides, wool, meat or labour; arable lands, vineyards and orchards, and fodder-bearing lands were worked by peasants who held their tenancies from the feudal landlords; forests and mines were both exploited by the state. The forests were handled by various government departments, depending on the final destination of the products, and it was their responsibility to see that all timber for beams, masts, floorboards and other building purposes, was hewn to the standards and measurements laid down by the architect Sinan, and that adequate stocks of wood and charcoal were prepared and delivered to fuel the capital and other cities. The mineral resources of Turkey, although considerable, were not exploited beyond the necessities of the state, and the vigilance of the government in limiting mining activities and setting out the rights and duties of miners was so thorough that they were not developed to anything like the profitable degree of which they were capable. When the presence of a valuable ore was reported, state surveyors went out to investigate and samples were sent for analysis. If the quality and potential were satisfactory, one or two villages neighbouring the site were declared exempt from taxation as compensation for enforced work in the mines. Experienced foremen were sent from other workings and operations were begun. Silver, copper, iron and even gold were mined, as well as saltpetre for explosives, and bullets were frequently cast on the spot near iron mines, and transported by bands of wandering Yuruks to the capital.

The lands held by the feudal landlords provided the livelihood of the peasantry of Anatolia, and were divided into holdings which were let out on a long-term basis to the tenant families who provided them with men-at-arms in time of war. A holding could be inherited by the tenant's son, or, on payment of a small sum, by certain close relatives. If there was no suitable heir the land was re-let to someone else; theoretically if it had been offered to and refused by all the peasants of the neighbourhood it could go to an outsider, but most village loyalties were so strong that it was rare for land to pass into the hands of a resident of another community. Indeed, free movement was discouraged except to take up vacant holdings, and the laws generally worked to bind the peasants to the soil; they reinforced established custom and insisted on its observance.

A single farm holding was measured by the area which could be worked by a pair of oxen. The holdings were worked by all the family, and as there were no particular privileges attached to primogeniture, on the death of the head of the household the inheritance was divided among all the heirs. Thus, although the eldest son assumed the responsibilities, especially that of maintaining dependent female relatives, the land itself was shared out, and many farms became smaller and less economic. Daughters received half as much as sons, and had to reside on the homestead they inherited, their husbands taking control; by judicious marriage arrangements between owners of adjacent strips, holdings could be re-aligned into larger and more productive units. Tenants were obliged to inform their feudal overlords of any changes, but if the land were properly cultivated, and all taxes and dues paid, families were never arbitrarily ejected from crown land. If, however, a tenant failed to work his holding he was fined in proportion to its size, and after three years of neglect the land was confiscated.

For taxation purposes, official registers were kept, and constantly brought up to date, of all animals, crops and bee-hives, and it was because all tax payments had to be made in coin that the peasants, for other purposes almost entirely independent of the urban population, took their goods to the nearest market to be sold to merchants for consumption by townspeople. Sometimes, when payment of taxes fell due at an inconvenient time, they were even obliged to come to disadvantageous arrangements with merchants, who advanced them money against the promise of delivery after the harvest. Where the feudal landlords maintained a close relationship with the peasants a valuable solidarity and understanding existed, but where taxes were farmed by Treasury contractors and no one defended the villagers' rights, they were often harshly exploited.

Much of the rural population lived in mountainous areas at some distance from the roads, where communications were little developed, and loyalties were in any case everywhere fiercely narrow; as a result village communities were almost completely self-supporting. All farm implements, such as ploughs, harrows and threshing sledges, were home-made, mostly of wood. From the flocks came not only the milk and milk products which, with the vegetables they grew, composed the peasants' diet, but also skins, leather, wool and hair. These were treated at home to produce the garments and shoes they wore, as well as their tents, carpets, saddlebags and blankets. Each household had a loom, and the women, accustomed to hard work of all kinds, had the task of carding, spinning, weaving, bleaching and dyeing. The men cured the skins and hides and made the leather equipment, as well as working with wood for the production of agricultural tools and of spoons and kitchen utensils. In winter the flocks were pastured near the villages in low-lying tracts of land; in the summer they were taken further afield, and the herdsmen who accompanied them lived with their animals for months, spending the nights in small tents, or brushwood shelters raised on stilts to catch a cooling breeze.

In spite of the great size of many flocks, the sheep were reared almost entirely for their wool; meat was seldom eaten and an animal was usually sold live only for the purpose of sacrifice. Much of the wool was used for the making of felt, a peasant craft. The fleece was spread over a frame, soaked with cauldrons of hot soapy water, and trodden down; this process was repeated until a felt of the required thickness was produced.

*69 Pack-mule bridge on the road to Mount Olympus. The domes and minarets of
Bursa can be distinguished on the left*

This was virtually indestructible, and the rugs and black nomad tents
and embroidered covers made from it were passed on as heirlooms.
From this felt were also made the shepherds' cloaks and hoods worn on
the chill mountain uplands, the knee-length cloaks worn by the cavalry,
snowboots, the characteristic hats of the Mevlevi dervishes, and dozens
of other everyday articles. The felt prayer rugs embroidered with silk and
gold thread were especially popular in the army, and all military
hammams were made of the fabric because it was equally impenetrable
by steam from within and cold from without. Even the Sultan and senior
officers used these tents, which for them were covered with linen and
lined inside with silk. The felt was also used, for its insulating properties,
to pack the snow which was cut into wedges on the mountains, especially
at Mount Olympus near Bursa, and sent down to the city by mule trains
continuously throughout the summer; the Palace had prior claim and
the rest of the snow was sold to the populace of Istanbul and other cities
for the cooling of sherbet and other drinks.

The fat-tailed sheep, which provided oil for cooking and lighting,
were the pride of certain flocks, and had tails which weighed eight to ten
pounds, or even more. The largest were carried behind the animal on a
little wheeled running-board, both because the weight was too much for
the beast and because the tail would be spoiled by being dragged about
the ground. The goats which produced the famous Angora mohair were

very carefully tended. The scanty dry grass which they seemed to enjoy produced a fleece far finer than that from animals fed on richer pastures. The goats were frequently washed in running water and their fine flossy hair, which reached the ground, was not sheared, but combed off in threads as delicate as silk. The women spun these into a workable yarn, which was then sent to Angora to be woven into fabric and dyed: green, the Prophet's colour, was most favoured, but white, orange, pale blue, violet and mouse-grey were considered lucky colours. But the distinctive feature of this fabric was the wavy design which appeared when it was subjected to a complicated process of dipping in water after being dyed. Cloth with large even waves was very highly esteemed, and worn by the wealthiest and most distinguished people.

Like the city-dwellers, the peasants were generally kind and reasonable with all their animals; although some were hunted for food, and others made to perform the same kind of monotonous hard work that they themselves were engaged on, there was nevertheless little wanton cruelty to helpless creatures, and even the poorest treated their animals with no less consideration than they showed their children. There were many stud farms and excellent veterinary surgeons. Horses were gently reared, without shouting or beating; they were covered with blankets at night, and the owners were as fastidious about pedigrees as they were thoughtful of the individual characters of their mounts. Mares were particularly highly valued and were tested for their sure-footedness by being ridden at speed down a steep mountain-side, on their closed, almost circular horse-shoes, to see whether they stumbled. In some provinces koumiss, which was made from fermented mare's milk, was widely drunk. Turks were very fond of cats, following the example of the Prophet who was said to have cut off the sleeve of his robe sooner than disturb the cat sleeping on it. The mosque gardens and streets were always full of cats, and several waqfs provided for their feeding. Turks were even kind to dogs, who were considered unclean beasts and frequently roamed the countryside in packs of strays. Their own sheep-dogs were fierce and loyal, utterly obedient to their master only, and totally fearless. A pure-bred animal could cost seven or eight times the price of a healthy boy slave in the Istanbul market, and the relationship between master and dog in the remote pasturages was such that they often ate out of one dish together. The dogs wore a wide leather collar set with iron spikes and there was no wild animal or threat to the flock that they were not prepared to attack. Mastiffs of this country breed were set loose to patrol outside army headquarters at night, and were the most effective possible deterrent to casual criminals.

Storks were particularly beloved, and nested on mosques and house-tops; they walked about fearlessly among the people, who respected them for possessing the virtue they themselves so much admired, of community responsibility. Small birds of all breeds nested safely among them, and the storks fed and protected the older birds who were no longer able to fend for themselves. In the autumn they waited preparatory to migration until the whole company had collected, before wheeling overhead at great height and setting off on their well-organised journey to Africa, during which they posted sentinels to guard the safety of the flock whenever they stopped for a rest. The Turks themselves continued to feed and care for the ones who could no longer travel with the main body in their great migration south.

The houses of most of the peasantry were little more than burrows in the hillside. The slope of the hill was cut away to make a perpendicular front, and the earth behind hollowed out to make a room. This excavated earth was piled up to make walls and roof for the front part, so that the room projected beyond the hillside, but grass soon covered the earth, so that only the front entrance was visible, and lambs grazed and children played on the turf of the roof. The innermost part of the house was the women's quarters; the cattle stable adjoined the main room in front and provided animal warmth on winter nights. The cooking stove was a huge earthenware jar partly sunk into the floor of the principal room, and in it was burned a mixture of chopped straw and animal dung. The cauldron was suspended by a chain from a bar over the mouth of the jar, and the smoke escaped with difficulty through a small aperture set high in the front wall. There was, as always, little furniture—a few carpets and quilts, and leather or woven bags, containing the clothes and household goods not in use, were hung on the walls or piled into corners. The floor was spread with kilims, which were rugs made of strips of woollen weaving of the kind used for saddle-bags, in bright colours and traditional regional patterns, sewn together to make the width required. In the store-room, which was partitioned off to one side, there was a tank for the making of boza, and jars for the storing of grain and of other food. The interiors of most homes, however poor, were generally clean, especially in the parts where food was kept or prepared.

The family ate squatting on the floor, or sitting cross-legged, and their diet consisted chiefly of bread and salt, eaten with leeks, onions and garlic, or turnips, parsnips and cucumber, and in addition yoghurt, cheese and fresh or dried fruits. Mutton or chicken with rice was a delicacy kept for celebrations, as were cakes, and sweet drinks of sherbet and grape-juice, and honey- or sugar-water.

Most families grew on their plots all the vegetables they needed, some of which were salted down for the winter; the autumn was a busy time of preparation for the lean months. The women made fuel-cakes of straw and dung; they beat the heaps of dry chick-pea plants with stout sticks, to free the grains from the pods; they brought in the grain harvest. Grain was spread on the ground for threshing, an ox or a couple of donkeys trampling over it, walking round and round in a circle drawing a threshing sledge. This was a flat tray of wooden boards, into which were set edgeways rows of sharp flints, which cut into the husks as they passed over them. Sometimes a child or a young girl sat on the sledge to give it more weight, but not so much as to tire the animal unnecessarily. The grain was then winnowed in big sieves, tossed up into the wind for the chaff to be blown away. The meal was originally ground in windmills, although Suleyman the Magnificent introduced horse-driven mills which were subsequently widely adopted throught the empire.

Although Anatolia was technically Muslim, religious belief in the countryside was always somewhat heterodox, and many practices retained clear traces of their pre-Islamic origins. In addition to the pagan survivals, there were areas strongly under the influence of various sects. As in the towns, the Bektashi movement owed much of its popularity to its free and cheerful social practices, and whole villages gave the sect their allegiance; elsewhere Mevlevi traditions might be strong. At the beginning of the year the 10th Muharrem, marked in some districts with solemn mourning, was celebrated in Shia villages with passion plays depicting the martyrdom of Huseyn, accompanied by fierce dancing and even bloodshed.

Some of the most satisfactory rituals combined the religious elements with the ancient customs. For example: the first forty of the coldest days of winter took their toll every year of the old and weak, and were followed by fifty days only slightly less cold and destructive, after which the survivors began to make preparations for a feast of thanksgiving and rejoicing. They made sacrifices, gave alms, offered up prayers of gratitude and then commemorated the end of the cruel winter with helva parties. These gatherings took place mainly in the guild rooms, and all sorts of sweet foods were eaten, especially a sweet made of dried apricots, almonds and cream, a rice dish sweetened with grape sugar, boza made of millet, and every kind of helva, which was basically a compound of either semolina or sesame and honey. The great moment of the celebration was the entry of the huge copper tray, on which was a mound of flour surrounded by a ring of sugar. Ten or twelve pastrycooks washed their hands, rolled up their sleeves and stood in a circle round the tray. There, hand on breast, and making a deep bow at every mention of the name of the Prophet, they recited a gulbenk, the invocation to God, concluding with the sonorous 'Hu-u-u-u-u'. The drums were beaten nine times, the 'Hu-u-u-u-u' repeated, and the drums beaten again. Then, to the accompaniment of songs, music and jokes, they plunged their hands into the flour, kneaded the sugar, and made the whole into a kind of spun sugar confection which was shared by all present. The eve of the spring festival always included the purifying ritual of jumping over fire, and also a kind of lucky dip of small objects which had been sealed into a jar, and which were drawn out one at a time to the accompaniment of appropriate verses, and distributed to those present.

There were few sophisticated amusements in the country, and the villagers provided their own, which consisted almost entirely of regional dances, or of rustic drama in which the women's parts were taken by men. They formed the entertainment which accompanied family celebrations of births, circumcisions and marriages, as well as the commemorations of seasonal changes and agricultural activities, both annual and occasional. These were usually accompanied by the collection of food from house to house, sometimes with music and dancing, to provide a feast of which the whole village partook. One such ceremony was rain-making, in which a boy or girl dressed in green leaves danced at each house while the inmates sprinkled water over the dancer's head. On the occasion of putting the rams to the ewes, a boy with bells round his waist danced through the streets of the village without speaking, and paused silently before each house, where he was given food for the subsequent feast. At the end of the rainy season young boys carrying burning torches and accompanied by a fiddler sang and danced in front of the houses, sometimes throwing a lighted torch through the door to symbolise the coming of the sun; other celebrations marked the end of the harvest or the passing of the winter solstice, which was accompanied by dances with a death and resuscitation theme, symbolising the re-awakening of the year. There were a number of provincial fairs which occurred seasonally in several areas and were of extremely ancient origin. Since some peasants came a great distance to participate, none lasted less than three days, and many went on for a week or more, and these unaccustomed concentrations of country people were guarded from brigands by soldiers deputed for that duty by the government. In addition to the display of agricultural products and local workmanship, a feature of these fairs was the dance and drama performances.

Regional dancing was not only a repository of local folk lore, but also one of the most important manifestations of village art, and if a leader felt that another dancer had come to surpass him in skill he resigned his position of authority to him. The dances were of great variety, some performed in a chain, some in line or semicircle holding hands or shoulders, some performed by one, or several at a time but independently. Men and women usually danced separately, and even in those districts where they danced together they were generally of the same family, and they never touched; they shared either a stick or a handkerchief. They performed in their best clothes, the women in their heirloom dress with silver belt and golden coins on their headgear, the men with embroidered bolero, sash and ornamented dagger, and trousers tight below the knee to display their neat footwork; all wore soft leather shoes. It was con-

70   Masked grotesque dancers with orchestra and audience

sidered indecent for hair to be allowed to show: women tied a scarf or
veil over their pillbox hat, and the men wore a small turban.

The dances were accompanied by songs from the dancers or audience,
or more usually by music from a shrill pipe and a large cylindrical drum,
hung from the shoulder and played with a small flexible stick in the left
hand and a larger hammer-headed stick to beat out the rhythm with the
right hand. Other instruments included primitive bag-pipes, a smaller
cylindrical drum for indoor use, a clay pot drum covered with sheepskin,
tambourines which were usually reserved for women's dances, kettle-
drums for certain religious and processional dancing, and the usual
wooden spoons and clappers. A number of the dances were mimetic.
Some imitated the actions of animals: the courtship of cranes, birds
sacred to the ancient Turks; an eagle approaching its prey; an encounter
between a dignified lion and a ferocious hyena; a clownish camel, danced
by two men in the animal's skin. Some imitated natural features, like
flowing water or swaying poplar trees; others mimed daily acts of home
and village life, like breadmaking, weaving or hair-washing; these were
interspersed with a promenading dance among the audience and always
ended with a lively dance of thanksgiving or favour-asking. But the most
popular were those, with or without weapons, that mimed battles or
fierce exploits, always intense and energetic, increasing in speed and
excitement and often ending with a leap over the flames of a fire. These
were the dances used when bringing a village bride to her new home.

There were also the religious dances. The Mevlevis learned from childhood to spin without getting giddy by holding a nail in the ground between two toes of a foot, and moving round this pivot. To the music of the flute, the dervishes began their whirling dance with their arms folded on their breast, hands clasping the opposite shoulder, and after spinning for a short while they flung their arms apart, the right raised above shoulder-level, hand open to receive the heavenly beneficence, the left drooping to the ground to allow it to pass through his body and return to nature. The two concentric circles of whirling dancers symbolised celestial motion, and the rotations reflected the cyclic sequence of the seasons. Members of the Alevi sect, too, danced in quasi-religious ceremonies, sometimes men and women together, never touching but moving in a slow mirror-dance; their religious leader was also the leader of the dance.

The dancing activities were widespread, and ancient in origin: with their roots in the old paganism, they included long-forgotten exorcism rites as well as acknowledgment of the forces of nature. The Islamic taboos on these practices were largely ignored by the peasantry, and even provoked a reaction which encouraged the dances as a form of defiance. The isolation of many villages provided an additional protection, and preserved the individuality and continuity of the forms, so that when, during the growth of the empire, groups of colonising Turks settled in the Balkans, they were able to take their strong dance traditions with them almost intact, and exerted a permanent influence on the dances of eastern Europe.

71 *Mevlevi dervish*

In addition to the feudal tenants, there were a number of tribal and minority peoples. The Yuruks were perhaps the largest indigenous group, with a number of sub-tribes of varied habits, mainly nomadic, and their encampments of black felt tents might be seen almost anywhere in Anatolia. Each tribe had a chief directly responsible to the central government. They spoke a variety of languages, all rough dialects of Turkish; some were Shia Muslims, some Sunni, and some had no formal religion; some were named for the natural colour or distinctive markings of their flocks, for example, the White

Sheep People and the People of the Black Goats; others were named after places of tribal ancestors. The Yuruks were a pastoral people, although in addition to the rearing of flocks some were engaged on wood-cutting and charcoal burning, and some entrusted with certain taks for the government, such as the transport of supplies across the country in the course of their seasonal wanderings. When the tribes moved their flocks from winter to summer quarters they were never allowed to stay longer than three days at any one stage, or to commit any depredation on waqf or feudal lands; their movements were observed by police who punished any breach of law immediately. They paid their tax, mainly in the form of fleeces, in the beginning of autumn, to the provincial governor of the district in which they had elected to make their summer camp, but provided they did not settle anywhere permanently the nomadic tribes paid no other regular dues. They were liable, however, to military service, sometimes replaced and sometimes supplemented by a cash contribution in time of war.

They were semi-sedentary in winter and built reed or wicker huts as an alternative to pitching their tents, which were large enough to hold the entire family of several generations. Inside either tent or hut their high wooden saddles were arranged to make a defensive wall, and the mattresses were rolled up against this during the day and spread on the floor at night. Their furniture was simple and portable: each household had a goatskin churn for making butter, and a loom for weaving kilims as well as cloth, but little more domestic equipment beyond a few jars and wooden plates and spoons, and a couple of heirloom copper pots. Occasionally travelling tinkers on their rounds tinned the pots and made whatever repairs might be necessary to harness or other metal articles, and in payment the tribe as a whole gave a muleload of cheese and butter. Their own diet was frugal: milk products and thin flat cakes of bread baked on copper plates over embers of dried dung, but they had high standards of hospitality.

Each wife had a separate tent and occupation, for example, two or three might tend goats or sheep, one looked after the camels, one fetched fuel and water, one made butter and cheese, one might be responsible for weaving. Although the Yuruks preferred to marry women of their own tribe, they did not hesitate to steal them from others when there was a shortage. The marriage rites were simple, celebrated with a meal made into a feast by the addition of meat—usually a lamb—and formalised with the exchange of handkerchiefs. The women bore many children, but large numbers died in infancy.

These tribes were polygamous, but the status of their women was relatively high, and in spite of the fact that they were unveiled the moral code was strictly observed.

Circumcision, when it was practised at all, was performed by a member of a sect not their own, sometimes even a Jew, and took place some days before the circumcision festivities themselves. To these a hoja was invited for the sake of appearances and given a token payment as though he had performed the operation, although in Islam it was not essentially a religious rite. The part removed at circumcision, like the placenta at birth, fallen teeth and nail parings, was always most carefully disposed of, as all of these could be powerful instruments of harm to the owner if they were used in a charm. Superstitious beliefs played a large part in their lives: burials took place near sacred trees which grew on the routes of their wanderings, and whenever they passed such a grave they threw on

72 Street of Greek houses in Izmir, with an unveiled woman at an open window

it a few stones from a heap near the tree, to which they added more stones, and tied rags or wooden spoons to the branches or to near-by bushes.

The large Christian population of Anatolia consisted mainly of members of the Greek Orthodox Church, many still living in communities which had been established in Byzantine times and had survived the Turkish migrations. In spite of the defeat of Byzantium the Christians of Asia Minor were not often forcibly converted to Islam, since, provided they were not dangerous, they were more useful to the Ottomans as payers of higher taxes; in fact some Christians voluntarily accepted Islam, in order to escape the disabilities to which non-Muslims were subject. On the other hand, in places where conversion had taken place the Christian religion was preserved and practised secretly. The Greek Orthodox millet was administered by the Patriarch in Istanbul; he and the bishops were drawn from the upper class of celibate clergy, but the village priests who tended to the simple religious needs of the village population were generally illiterate, humble and little respected. They were allowed to marry, and as they frequently had many children and depended for their livelihood on contributions from their parish, they were miserably poor. In those villages where Christians and Muslims lived side by side, there was, as with the popular religion of all simple peasant peoples, considerable interchange of worship in holy places. The Greeks of Anatolia were cheerful, light-hearted and buoyant people, sometimes even rash and hasty, all characteristics not common to their Turkish neighbours. Their manners and customs differed little, essentially, from those in the Greek provinces of the empire.

Although there had been Jewish communities in Asia Minor since Byzantine times, and probably earlier, the Jews of Turkey were predominantly Sephardi, refugees from the Spanish Inquisition who spoke a dialect of Spanish, using Hebrew only for religious purposes. In 1666, one of their number, Sabbatai Zevi, professed Islam after having proclaimed himself Messiah in Salonika; his followers also became nominal apostates and lived as Turks, but continued secretly in the Jewish faith, meeting privately in certain windowless houses to practise their religion, and marrying only among themselves. These dönmes, as the sect was called—the word means 'turning'—were objects of suspicion to both Jews and Muslims. Few Jews made their homes in the countryside; most engaged in trade or such professions as medicine, in the towns.

The gipsies who roamed in small bands over Anatolia were despised by the Muslims, whom in turn they hated. In the towns and villages the men led performing bears and monkeys, and the women told fortunes. They were skilled in the making of medicines and potions from plants and herbs; their younger girls were much in demand for singing and dancing at weddings and parties; their men were gifted in the management of horses, and able metal-workers, but they remained poor, wild and lawless, with little formal religion and few traditional ceremonies.

The great roads of Anatolia led from the capital to the major cities and thence to the eastern parts of the empire. They were narrow paved tracks, three feet wide to allow for the passage of horsemen, with paths on either side for pedestrians and flocks. The main traffic was caravans of camels and mules carrying provisions from the provinces to Istanbul, army convoys, and flocks and herds.

The military caravans and convoys were enormous and always well-supplied with all necessities, since in some embattled areas the retreating local armies practised a burnt-earth policy and fired houses and barns, leaving no food for the pursuing troops. Although, therefore, they supplemented their stocks with whatever could be foraged on the way, they were always adequately prepared for long marches and campaigns without reinforcement of supplies if necessary. Officers' food and equipment were carried on baggage mules and camels; the men of the cavalry troops each had a sumpter horse carrying food, clothes, bedding and canvas for a tent, led on a halter by a man-at-arms; supplies for the soldiery travelled by cart. When the Sultan moved camp, a not un-familiar sight was the line of soldiers whose horses had been killed in battle: the men stood by the roadside with their saddles on their heads, and at his discretion the Sultan would make an allowance for the purchase of fresh horses for them.

The trading caravans varied in size, and the dates of departure and arrival were fixed in order to avoid the appearance of too many goods at once, which would flood the market and affect prices. There were some, however, which had a regular timetable: a camel and horse caravan passed between Izmir and Istanbul every week; the caravans between the capital and Georgia left every three months; there were two a year from Basra, three or four from Aleppo and between six and ten from Persia. The times taken varied, depending on the size of the caravan, the speed of the slowest participant and the conditions of the road at different times of the year; thus, the caravan from Izmir might take between ten and twenty days, and that from Persia between two and three months. In hot arid country the caravans travelled in the cool of the night, reaching their resting-places at dawn; indeed, the Turkish name for the morning star was 'Kervan kiran'—'Caravan-breaking'—because it marked the temporary dispersal of the train of travellers and their animals. The halts might take place at one of the main crossroad towns, where the composition of the caravan could change and new groups form to continue the journeys, or they might occur along the roads, where, at the intervals of twenty to twenty-five miles which made up a day's journey, stood the famous khans, or caravanserais. Sometimes the focus of a small village that grew up under its protec-

73   *Khan at Guzelhisar in Anatolia*

tion, sometimes isolated on the bleak plateau, the roadside khans offered, within their fortified walls, safe and dependable lodgings as well as a variety of facilities. They were available to travellers, pilgrims, merchants, postal convoys; all those on the road, in fact, with the exception of soldiers on the march, who made their own camps. All the exterior decoration of the khans was concentrated on the gateways, in which were set great double doors of wood covered with iron plates secured with huge-headed nails; in one door was a small wicket-gate, through which men could pass singly, while the doorkeeper lived by the entrance and kept watch on all who went in and out. In the simpler khans there was little privacy. The open courtyard in the centre was used for the animals, baggage and wagons. Set against the wall that surrounded it was a ledge, about three feet above the ground and four feet deep, with a number of hearths on it, and here the travellers made their little encampments, singly or in small groups. They cooked their meal on the fireplace against the wall, and slept on a rug with their saddle for a pillow and a cloak for a blanket, and the animals tethered at the foot of their master's pitch would put their heads over the ledge for a crust or a piece of turnip. But the large splendid khans provided separate private rooms with hearths, as well as dormitories, bathrooms and lavatories; around the open courtyard in which the animals were tethered were also the arched, vaulted storerooms for baggage and fodder, and beyond it a covered hall for the animals' winter quarters, the domed roof pierced for light and ventilation. In hot regions, a stairway led up to a flat roof where the travellers assembled and ate in the evening before the caravan moved off. In the centre of the courtyard, or over one of the rooms around it, was a small mosque, and by the gateway were a coffee-room, a repair shop for vehicles, a smithy and stables.

The majority of the finest old khans, single-storey buildings faced with cut stone, were built in the thirteenth century, and many remained in continuous use for hundreds of years. The later Ottoman khans, more usually found in the towns, usually had two storeys, and were built of brick or stone, with lead-covered roofs; on the lower floor were the shops and store-rooms and a small mosque; on the upper were the living rooms. In the large cross-road towns were also to be found some extremely well-appointed hostels, used by provincial governors and high-ranking military officers travelling on government business. Endowed by waqf, these provided in addition to free accommodation and other facilities an evening meal, usually a large wooden platter holding a dish of pilaff made of cracked wheat or barley and a little stewed meat, with loaves of bread and sometimes a comb of honey.

9

The Provinces

Most of the rules governing the administration of provinces were originally framed for Rumelia and Anatolia, but some of the territories acquired during the expansion of the empire consisted of larger and more loosely knit groupings, and in any case distinction had to be made between Muslim lands brought under Ottoman control, and Christian states conquered according to the original principle of warring against the infidel. In the Muslim Asiatic provinces Ottoman rule was on the whole superficial, and tended to make few modifications in the systems which already prevailed; the Christian dependencies on the other hand were more strictly administered. They were, however, allowed freedom of religious practice and internal government, provided they paid the required taxes and respected the rules which had been laid down for the government of such territories. Principally, they were required to accept Muslim supremacy and to show no disrespect or hostility; they were also obliged to entertain and maintain at their expense Muslim officials or travellers who were passing through their communities, and, of course, to accept the periodic levy of Devshirme boys. In exchange the Ottoman government guaranteed security of lives and property as well as of religious rights.

In a number of Christian dependencies, particularly the Balkans and eastern Europe, the coming of the Turks meant an improvement in living conditions and particularly in communications, as trade routes were expanded by land and river to the capital, Istanbul. In addition, the hold of many feudal landlords was broken, and the division and redistribution of their land among the peasant population inspired both gratitude and co-operation, and thence the progress consequent on good relations. But, as in all mainly rural communities, the effects of administrative changes were almost imperceptible, and on the whole life continued along the traditional patterns of the various peoples. The village headman, the priest, the smith, the old woman who brewed herbs and made up spells, all pursued unchanged their rôles in the affairs of their communities.

In addition to the population of the Greek islands and mainland, and the Greek villages in Asia Minor, there were numbers of their settlements scattered about the empire, seldom shared with villagers of any other race, and always demonstrating a high degree of adherence to common beliefs and customs. There were everywhere reminders of their pre-Christian affiliations to pagan gods in their extreme superstitious reverence and placatory attitude towards storms, mountains and all phenomena of nature, and there was something less than religious in their annual festivals of saints that were celebrated with village fairs. Pilgrims who had come from a distance to visit a saint's tomb frequently spent the night camped in the church; their votive offerings of small gold coins stuck to the cheeks of the statue of the Virgin were considered ample compensation by the poor priests who guarded the shrine. The details of the celebration of family occasions, holy days and traditional festivities varied comparatively little from region to region, and almost all demonstrated to some degree an ancient confusion of religious reverence and superstitious dread. On the birth of a baby both mother and child were considered to be so vulnerable to the attacks of malign spirits that they were never left alone until after the infant was baptised, and so rendered safe. Their dead were buried with great grief and lamentation, assisted by professional mourners, and forty days later a commemorative feast was eaten at the grave, with candles to carry prayers for the soul of the departed; after three years the body was exhumed and the bones thrown on a charnel heap. Certain religious festivals, such as Lent, were rigorously observed, especially by the women. On the Thursday before Easter the housewife baked sweet cakes and boiled coloured eggs, usually red, one for each member of the family and one or two extra, and these she took to church where they were left in the aura of sanctity. The service on Friday evening was celebrated with the utmost solemnity, as the holiest day in the Orthodox year, concluding with the priest lighting a taper from the lamp burning before the ikon and offering it to the nearest congregants, who passed the light on to others, and so on through the church until it was ablaze with candle flames, symbolic of the rebirth of Christ. On Easter Sunday the family ate the sweet cakes and broke and shared the eggs, but the extra eggs were put away and kept for the rest of the year, to be brought out in case of illness to effect cures with their divine or magic powers. Other religious holidays and traditional festivals were celebrated with feasting and dancing; the most general favourite was St. George's Day, which marked the beginning of Spring and also the eating of fresh meat, since traditionally no lambs were slaughtered each year until that date. The peasant Greeks lived by sheep-rearing and such agriculture as their land permitted; their women, married by the age of twelve or thirteen, worked on the farms and at their spinning and weaving, but not usually at the sowing and harvesting in the fields. There were many sponge divers among the island Greeks; they had a technique of filling the mouth with oil and diving very deep, then releasing the oil to form bubbles which acted as clear lenses in the gloomy depths. Many made their living by fishing, and they were fearless seamen although the sudden storms in the Aegean provided many hazards for their small craft. Greek peasant life was everywhere frugal and hard, but they were a cheerful and active people, high-spirited to the point of recklessness, moody, but with a sense of humour as well as of honour.

The Albanians, on the other hands, were a harsh and dour people. Their small towns were dreary, with mean, poor streets and shops, and even the two-storey houses of the wealthier families were gloomy and austere; the mountain headquarters of the provincial governors were bleak remote fortresses. The villages consisted of poorly furnished cottages containing one living-room and one store-room, the gardens surrounded by a high wall. Each village had a communal threshing-floor on which the grain was trodden out by horses. Both men and women were extraordinarily brave, and participated regardless of sex in the terrible blood feuds that raged between individuals and families, and sometimes between whole villages or even clans. Women were much respected, and even if they had adopted the Muslim religion went unveiled in the country. A strict moral code prevailed, and adultery was punished with immediate death. There was much marrying between clans, and some mountain tribes were even bold enough to raid Muslim villages and steal their women, a situation which, after some face-saving indignation, was usually accepted on payment of a dowry. They feared only the supernatural, and lived in superstitious dread of unseen powers. They believed that all illnesses were caused by malign influences, and that shadows could assume independent existence for evil purposes. Travellers placed stones in the forks and hollows of roadside trees to placate restless spirits, so that they could go safely on their way, and, particularly in the mountains, there were many fire ceremonies with burning logs for the appeasement of ancient gods. They swore 'by sky and earth', 'by mountain and plain', 'by sun and moon' and, picking up a stone, 'by this weight'. They had no art or written literature, but the stories of their tribes were commemorated in long ballads sung round the fire on winter evenings. The men were mainly soldiers, traders, woodcutters or shepherds, and the women did all the other work on the land in addition to the housework, bread-making, churning, brewing, spinning, weaving and the dozens of other domestic tasks, all performed in primitive conditions. Marriages were arranged by the women of the family, who were usually best informed of the degrees of kinship and descent of all likely young candidates. They chose a bride for a marriageable son and settled all preliminaries, and on payment of dowry and a joint celebration the bride was brought to the father's house and added to the patriarchal family. As in Greece, funerals were accompanied by screaming and wailing; the men surrounded the bier on the way to the burial and the women walked behind, and as the body was laid in bare earth and covered with a stone slab they moaned and rocked, falling silent only at the arrival of the dish of boiled wheat with dried fruit and spices that was eaten as a memorial feast. When a member of the tribe met his death away from home, this feast was eaten in his honour even though there had been no burial, and close relatives wore their coats inside out as a sign of mourning.

The town life of the Bulgars was similar to that of the Greeks, but life in the country was freer for them than for Greek peasants. The women were equal in respect and work with the husbands and fathers, and did not marry so young. A young husband was not obliged to live under the paternal roof but was allowed to build a small cottage on his father's land, although of course he continued to work for him. The better houses were built of stone, and the poorer families built a framework of poles laid over with wattles and plastered thickly inside and out with clay and a mixture of cow-dung and straw. The walls were whitewashed, and the arched roof which projected like a porch over the entrance was thatched or occasionally tiled. The accommodation inside consisted of a common living-room with a big fireplace, a family bedroom and a store-room, and the earth floor was covered with thick woollen mats on which the family sat to eat and slept at night. Each house had its ikon in a corner, with a tiny oil lamp suspended before it, some shelves with a few pots and plates, a loom and a spinning wheel, and in the corners were piled the bundles of bedding and clothes. The animals and fodder were kept outside, in sheds or wicker enclosures. The houses were clean, and their lives, although simple and economical, not uncomfortable; they ate mainly rye bread and beans and dairy produce, and on festive occasions celebrated with pig or lamb and a sort of sweet heavy cake, and drank home-made wine. Everyone worked hard; in addition to their pastoral and agricultural tasks they grew and picked the acres of roses to be made into the famous essence and rose-water. After the grape vintage and the harvest were safely in, when the work had slackened off a little, was the season of weddings, and parents bought wives for their sons. When the transaction had been satisfactorily concluded between the families, the bride, her wedding dress covered with ornaments and coins, was led by her father to the groom's house accompanied by her family and friends, the whole party on horseback. There the entire village joined in the wedding feast. Indeed they needed little encouragement, for unlike the Greeks who could only celebrate when the mood was upon them, the Bulgars were ready to dance at any time to the sound of bagpipes or to a sung accompaniment. They had a fatalistic attitude towards death, and their funerals were restrained; the women made some demonstration of grief but were more concerned to turn their pots and pans upside-down so that the departing spirit would not take refuge in them and thereafter haunt the house. The corpse was dressed in holiday clothes and laid on a pillow filled with earth; an ikon was laid on his breast and flowers placed around the bier. Friends came to say a last farewell and to bring flowers and candles with messages for him to deliver to their own departed. All this was carried on an ox-cart to the grave-side, where, after a funeral meal of bread and wine, the body was undressed, wrapped in a shroud and buried in a coffin, and the women returned home to clean the house thoroughly and remove any traces of an unquiet spirit. The obligatory holy days of the year were duly observed, with particular scrupulousness over the fast of Lent culminating in the devotions of Easter, but, as in Greece, each village had its old wise woman whose power was far greater than that of the village priest.

The Wallachians were an almost entirely pastoral people. In winter they made their homes in the mountain villages; sometimes half under-ground and covered with rough thatch, looking like nothing so much as dunghills; sometimes perched in the trees, where they also kept their haystacks, out of the reach of straying animals. For the rest of the year they wandered in communities with their flocks and herds. The women cared for the animals, and carded, spun, knitted and wove; when they could go down into the few poor towns they sold their produce in the markets and with the proceeds bought coarse silver jewellery both as an adornment and a form of saving.

For these, and many other Balkan peoples, life was a monotonous round of early rising, hard work and frugal diet; the routine was broken by simple pleasures eagerly anticipated and enjoyed in a spirit of com-mon rejoicing, or, more sombrely, by the arrival of the officials from Istanbul for the collection of young boys, and the grief of loss they left behind them. Many areas were also sorely tried by the insatiable demands of Janissary troops, who exacted board and lodging from the unfortunate peasants on whom they billeted themselves during journeys to and from campaign, and who had the additional insolence to demand their notorious 'tooth-rent'. Apart from these dreaded interruptions they pursued the occupations of the various seasons; their tools and methods of husbandry·were primitive and traditional, but adequate to the feeding and maintenance of themselves and their livestock. Houses were ill-lit; their day started early and the work was hard, and after the evening meal there was little to keep them from their beds. Toilet and washing facilities were primitive, but their rough life had bred a hardy people and their food, although sparse, was healthy. In any case, skilled medical attention was non-existent, and most villagers combined a strong spirit of self-dependence with a high degree of fatalism.

The everyday working dress was usually of coarse brown woollen material or, in winter in the mountains, of sheepskins. The men wore an open wool or skin jacket, with the sleeves hanging loose, over a coarse knee-length shirt and wide trousers tight at the ankle. The women wore a jacket over a smock and calf-length skirt, and both were often barefoot, or wore heavy boots. Their holiday clothes, however, of bright dyed materials, braided and embroidered, and worn at marriages and on festive occasions, varied not only from country to country but also from district to district, in traditional patterns that were jealously guarded and inherited with pride.

The Armenians were the largest Christian group in Asiatic Turkey; Mount Ararat on which Noah's Ark traditionally landed was in their ancestral lands. Like the Greeks, they had a higher clergy of bachelors or, occasionally, widowers, and a poor inferior clergy of little rank. The churches in their towns were finely decorated outside with high-relief carvings of trees and animals, biblical figures and allegorical scenes. Their dwellings were gloomy and cheerless: the peasants lived in hovels excavated in the mountainside, and the better-class in mud-brick houses

74 Detail of biblical carvings on the wall of the Armenian church of Aght'amar at Van. Lower left: Jonah thrown to the whale

with white-washed walls and sometimes carved and painted wooden ceilings. They dressed in layers of hard-wearing, brightly-coloured garments, shedding or adding to them according to the season, although a number adopted the dress of the Turks of Asia Minor when for purposes of trade they settled in Turkish towns. Armenian women had the reputation of being neat, clean and industrious: they spun and wove handsome materials, especially a heavy silk brocade patterned with flowers, and made good white felt, and the older women were famous for their orange- and rose-flower water and preserves.

Families lived in patriarchal units of three or four generations under one roof, and although children were loved and even indulged, family discipline was strong. Marriages were contracted young—twelve years of age was usual for a girl—and divorce was impossible. The wedding celebrations lasted for several days, and an important functionary at these, and on all festive occasions, was the village barber, who on the wedding day would spend the morning shaving the groom in the presence of his friends, prolonging the operation with the telling of jokes and stories. When the guests considered the performance had gone on long enough they gave him small gifts of money and he concluded his work, and gave the signal for the dressing of the groom. The party of men then moved off to the bride's house, wearing scimitars in symbolism of snatching the girl away against her will; there, after an exchange of greetings between the two families, the bride was blindfolded and led to the church, which had been decorated by the bride's friends with garlands of flowers. After the religious ceremony the couple left for the wedding feast to the accompaniment of songs and the throwing of corn and small coins; the bride, wearing a silver plate on her head tied with a long wrap of crimson silk, led off the dance with her father. Forty days after the wedding the bride was allowed to go to the well for the first time, and this was the occasion for a small celebration among the women. Until she had given birth to a male child, a young bride wore a red woollen veil and was permitted to address only those relatives in the household who were junior to herself, and to speak to her husband in his parents' presence only with the patriarch's permission. As with the Greeks, when a child was born neither mother nor baby was left alone for an instant until after the baptism service, for fear of malign influences.

Although their native intelligence and natural aptitude encouraged a number to set up successfully in business in Turkish communities as bankers and merchants, most Armenians pursued the occupations of the countryside as farmers and herdsmen, thrifty and hard-working, taxed as were all the Christian millets, law-abiding and reasonable. They were, however, in a permanent state of feud with the Kurds, their neighbours.

The Kurds, of whom there were many tribes, were numbered, for tax purposes, by tents, each of which contained between five and twenty inhabitants. The life of the nomadic Kurds was dictated by their pasturage; the men guarded the flocks, mainly of sheep, and moved about the countryside from one watered feeding-area to another, while the women undertook all other duties. Their animals were too valuable to use for meat and their diet consisted of pilaff made of cracked wheat, and dairy products: milk, cheeses and yoghurt, and butter made in a sheepskin slung horizontally by the feet and rocked to and fro, a task for young girls. When the tribe moved, the men went ahead driving the animals, and the women, unveiled, fearless and competent, followed with the baggage on bullocks, pitching and striking their own camps on the way. These strong-minded women chose their husbands themselves, or ran away with the man of their choice if permission were withheld, which was seldom. They managed every aspect of the community's life: when he caught up with the tribe their husbands even referred the tax-collector to them, and they made his task almost impossible, hiding taxable goods in places he dare not search and screaming and railing at his demands, while the men of the family stood around shrugging their shoulders and saying: 'You see what a life we have to lead.' In their internal dealings, however, the Kurds had a very high standard of dignity and morality, and any breach of tribal custom or ethics was followed by quick vengeance. They were monogamous, and divorce among them was rare. The betrothal ceremony was celebrated with a feast at which the groom was represented by a brother or near male relative; it was followed by a wedding dance at which as many as possible of the tribe were present, and this constituted a binding marriage.

There were some sedentary Kurds whose small towns provided a market-place for the nomads. Their simple square single-storey houses were made of sun-dried bricks covered with a plaster made of mud and straw, the flat rafters of the roof laid over with reeds and earth. The chief room was the entrance hall, open in front and used in summer for eating and sleeping; poorer people slept on the flat roof of their mud huts. They were, not unnaturally, somewhat more law-abiding; although often poorer they paid their dues with rather less argument, and exchanged a verbal contract before their imam on the occasion of a marriage.

Scattered among the Kurds were found members of a strange religious group called the Yezidis, who believed that God had entrusted the world to seven angels, the chief of them being the Peacock Angel, a name they were forbidden to speak aloud. He had fallen from Paradise but had subsequently repented; the tears he shed for 7000 years had put out the flames of hell. The Yezidis denied the existence of evil, but because they were known to revere a power other than Allah they were regarded by others as devil-worshippers, and although the Muslims despised them they sometimes consulted their priests because of their reputedly supernatural powers.

Theoretically the general land organisation of the Arab provinces was simple: some lands were devoted to waqf endowments and some were held by a tenant-in-chief but sub-let to smaller farmers, who paid their tax to him and could not be evicted save for non-payment. The details of land-holding, however, were extremely complicated, and the rights and usages differed widely from one area to another. All these methods were adapted into the flexible Ottoman system and traditional practice was seldom interfered with; indeed, any attempt to introduce new methods would have been doomed to failure.

The peasants of the Arab provinces were miserable and downtrodden, with a very low standard of living. Long before the Ottoman conquests they had become accustomed to gross exploitation by their landlords, and their bitter resignation to their harsh living conditions was compounded by the apathy caused by physical under-nourishment. Their cultivated lands were constantly ravaged by the Bedouin nomads, who raided them mercilessly or demanded protection money as insurance for crops and livestock. The semi-settled Bedouin took by force the best grazing grounds, diverted water courses for their own use, and even seized the harvest of other villages if their own had been neglected during their absence at war. The peasants' agricultural methods and implements were extremely primitive, partly because of lack of incentive to improve on the barely adequate old ways, since any suggestion of innovation was regarded with suspicion as a means of trying to get more work out of them, and partly because of a deep-rooted overpowering inability to depart from accepted custom in any form.

Villages were self-contained and self-governing, and their relations with the central government were generally limited to the payment of taxes. The principal sheikh of each village or group acted as magistrate and arbiter, and imposed the law with stern justice which was accepted without question. Each village had one or two shopkeepers and potters and the few artisans needed to make or repair the articles of everyday use for their simple needs; in addition it supported, out of its own resources, an imam for the mosque and Koran school, a barber and a carpenter, and guards for the protection of crops and granaries, to give warning of the approach of Bedouin marauders and to patrol irrigation ditches and boundaries. Sons followed fathers in their occupation, and daughters as far as possible married men of their father's trade. Each community remained tightly-knit and there was little peaceful contact between the groups, whether village or nomadic; their relations with the central government were conducted through their sheikh. Little stock was raised; the farmers with larger holdings had a few oxen and buffaloes for their ploughing and other field operations, and when they needed to transport their goods to market they hired camels from the Bedouin, part of whose power lay in the fact that they were the almost exclusive suppli-

75   *Bedouin women with handmill*

ers of these beasts which were, in turn, the main means of transport of
caravans and merchandise. The peasants owned one or two asses, and
sometimes a few goats for milk and for making into water-skins. Pigeons
were an important free source of food and also of manure, which was
collected carefully for use on crops since the dung of larger beasts, when
mixed with chopped straw, was almost the only source of fuel and as such
far too precious to be spread on the soil. The main industries supplied by
the labour of the peasants were the manufacture of cotton, linen and
other textiles; the production of silk in particular supported several
ancillary trades such as dyeing, embroidery, and tassel-making. They
also produced the raw materials for mats and carpets, oil and oil products, soap, soda and candles, loaf sugar and molasses, salt, saltpetre and
sal-ammoniac from the mines, and in addition, both for consumption
within the country and for export, grain, fodder, root crops and fruit.
Most land bore two crops annually, some even three, but the peasants,

189

feudally bound and without redress, had no share in these resources. Their diet consisted of bread, salt fish, a few vegetables, the small eggs of half-starved hens and a little milk. Their dress was a single smock-like garment, with a woollen wrap and a head shawl. The women worked harder than the men, grinding corn for bread, fetching water sometimes from a distance, and making dung cakes for fuel, as well as labouring in the fields. The marriage arrangements were usually extremely simple, and it was enough for a woman to say, without witnesses, 'I give myself up to thee', and no marriage contract or certificate was necessary. This made the position of women extremely precarious, and wives unable to work hard enough lived in constant fear of divorce. On the other hand the moral code was rigid, and if a woman proved unfaithful her family considered themselves more disgraced than her husband and would immediately band together to kill her, either by cutting her into pieces or by drowning her in a river with a stone round her neck.

One of the most powerful peoples was the Bedouin. In addition to the breeding of camels and cultivation of crops, they had enormous mixed herds of sheep and goats, and supplied wool, mutton, butter, cheese and camel hair to local town markets as well as reeds, alkali and farm produce, but their overwhelming preoccupation was the constant pursuance of civil war among themselves. Rivalry over grazing grounds or irrigation rights, real or fancied personal insults, a murder to be avenged, any reason was enough to plunge whole tribes into bloody warfare in which there was no place for scruples of religion or humanity, and no consideration of economic or political consequences. Rivalries between families, groups and tribes were of overriding importance and took precedence over personal preference or standards of morality, and the Turkish government was unable to maintain order among them and found it difficult to give their victims much protection. Occasionally they managed to persuade a tribe, by paying it well, to police a trade route instead of raiding it, for only Bedouin could deal with Bedouin. To protect parts of the route to Mecca, certain chiefs were made responsible for the safety of pilgrims passing through their territory and were rewarded by an official appointment or exemption from taxation, but generally they were as hostile to Turkish authority as they were refractory among themselves.

The Bedouin were not the only turbulent tribesmen: the Druzes of Palestine, Syria and Lebanon, as well as the Turcomans of northern Syria and the Kurds of Eastern Turkey and Iraq were a constant source of anxiety. Many of these peoples, either because of the extreme inaccessibility of their territory, or their nomadic habits, or sometimes because of their intractable temper, were virtually autonomous and considered that they owed allegiance only to their chief. The regulations of the central government either never reached them or were disregarded as much as possible, and the Ottomans were wise enough to content themselves with the collection, as far as they were able, of any taxes they could impose on these unsubjugatable peoples. The administration of law and formal punishment was almost impossible, and most tribesmen had their own simple rules. By these, death was punished by death, that is to say, a free man died for a free man, a slave for a slave, a woman for a woman; sometimes the murderer paid blood-money to the heirs of the deceased, which was divided among them according to their laws of inheritance. This blood price was a debt incumbent on the tribe or family, and retaliation for wounds and mutilations was based on it; thus, for cutting off a man's hand the price was one-half of that for his death, and for a finger the price was one-tenth. For the theft of an object which had not been too easily accessible the right hand was cut off for a first offence, for a second the left foot, for a third the left hand and for a fourth the right foot; there was no penalty for the theft of perishable food. Four eye-witnesses were necessary for proof of adultery, and if the woman were convicted she was killed by stoning. Unintentional homicide was redeemed by the setting free of a Muslim slave and the payment of a fine to the family of the dead man, and if the murderer were unable to free a Muslim he was obliged to fast for two months; it was recognised that a man might kill in self-defence or in defence of his property.

On the whole the Ottoman government was not unduly oppressive, and the administration reasonably honest, but as the centre of power was far away, and some provincial governors proved weak or corrupt, it was hopelessly difficult to establish a satisfactory system of rule. The tribesmen themselves were impossible to please: they despised any assertion of power that was not accompanied by harshness and violence, yet where they felt that there had been a lack of liberality and magnanimity in their rulers, or where some unwritten law had been violated, they did not hesitate to rise in vengeance. Although in theory only members of the standing and feudal armies were allowed firearms, the tribesmen were able to procure almost unlimited supplies from a variety of smuggled sources. Besides those which were sold directly by soldiers for ready money, a small thriving trade was conducted by fief-holders and minor officials who conspired to sell wheat to Franks in exchange for arms, which they passed on at a price of two or three gold pieces for each musket. This was doubly illegal, since, besides the restrictions on arms, the sale of wheat outside the empire was forbidden.

In the face of this armed opposition most competent Turkish governors, if they could not play off one faction against another, maintained a totally neutral attitude to the violent feuds, and gained what esteem they could by the construction and repair of such public works as canals, khans and religious buildings. On the major highways, especially on the roads to the holy cities of Mecca, Jerusalem and Hebron, they established fortified caravanserais which not only afforded security to pilgrims and traders but also acted as military bases, although of limited effectiveness. Sometimes in the vicinity of these, and sometimes at crossroads in un-inhabited parts of the country, they also founded settlements by taking families from villages in the surrounding area, to a total of between forty and 200 households, according to the danger of the locality. These new villages were obliged to police the area, and some became the nuclei of little towns in which, eventually, public buildings were constructed and regular markets held. Administrative authority in the wilder regions, however, remained precarious.

Not all tribes were rebellious: the Tatars, Muslims who came from south Russia, were a Mongol people who roamed with their flocks and, like the Yuruks of Anatolia, fulfilled certain obligations imposed by the central government. They were a quiet, honest, sober people, thrifty and industrious although very dirty in their dress and food, in which they used a great deal of rancid mutton fat. During the summer they roamed mainly in the mountains of northern Persia and eastern Turkey, and in addition to caring for their sheep they were great bee-keepers, carrying their hives of hollow segments of tree-trunk with them on their wander-ings. Their encampments, often among ruins and wayside tombs, were guarded by fierce dogs; in winter they built small settlements of simple two-room huts made of reeds and clay. Their domestic articles were mainly of wood, which they turned with great skill. Their great enter-tainment was to tell and listen to long stories of tribal heroes and historical events: they were descendants of the Golden Horde and the ancestor of their ruling house was Genghis Khan himself. Both men and women excelled in horsemanship, and one of the customs of their wedding ceremony was the departure of the bride, enveloped in a scarlet veil, on horseback from her father's home and accompanied by her party. The groom and his men rode out to meet her, and from the moment they saw each other the two groups approached in absolute silence, until, without warning, when the groom considered he was near enough, he threw an apple or an orange at the bride and confusion immediately broke out. The groom whirled his horse round and dashed for home, with the bride's horsemen in hot pursuit. If they caught him before he reached his tent he forfeited his horse, saddle and clothes, which he had to redeem with silver coins. When the bride reached his tent her women surrounded her and pretended to beg her not to dismount, while his family rode round and round the group pleading with her to get down and give them all wedding gifts. Eventually the marriage was concluded with feasting and dancing.

The sedentary populations of the cities of the eastern provinces were more accessible to the attentions of Turkish officials, but even there con-trol was mainly indirect. They were composed of small, self-contained and almost autonomous units, each with its own mosque, bath and local market, and with gates which were closed at nightfall. They were separated from each other by the large main markets, or souks, which crossed the city. The general responsibility for policing the cities was shared by the agha of the local corps of Janissaries and the market superintendent; as in Turkey, the market inspectors played an important part in the maintenance of public order. They patrolled the streets preceded by an officer with measuring scales and followed by executioners and other servants. They tested the scales, weights and measures in shops and markets, asked the prices of goods, sometimes stopping customers to enquire about their purchases, and on the discovery of any defection the guilty shopkeeper was punished on the spot, usually by flogging.

As in Turkey, the importance of the trade guilds was impossible to over-estimate, and through them the humblest citizen could play a part in the social, and even political, life of the group. The sheikhs who represented the guilds in their relations with the government, and were responsible for the collection and payment of taxes, also provided a channel through which the administration could maintain order and exercise discipline. Even the guild of thieves was obliged to give satisfaction through their sheikh to any offended party whose complaint was important enough to pass through official channels.

The various groups, whether of trade, residence, religion or any other tie, occasionally overlapped, but each possessed a homogeneous and separate unity and received exclusive allegiance. There was occasionally some organisation for common action, for example for participation in religious festivals, or for joint guild displays in the processions that marked such festivities as for the accession of a new Sultan; it might also be necessary to call out all citizens for the defence of the city in an emergency. But there were no municipal institutions, and any spontaneous association between groups would be regarded by the authorities with the gravest suspicion.

The urban poor lodged over shops or in hovels of unbaked bricks cemented with mud, the roof of palm branches laid over rafters and covered with a plaster of mud and straw. Each family unit consisted of one or two rooms in which the family lived and slept, and a kitchen and latrine; at the far end opposite the entrance was a stove on which they slept in the winter. The only furniture was a mat or two, a few earthen vessels and a hand-mill for the corn which was ground every day to make the bread. For many, living conditions were little better than those of the feudal peasants, and some families were so destitute that they sold their children or left them at the door of the mosque, usually at the time of the Friday noon prayer, in the hope that some pious man might take them home even temporarily. Many women worked as servants and labourers for very little pay, and ate even less than the men; their dress was rags.

The better houses were built so that their windows did not overlook the private quarters of other families, and in the summer many people slept on the roof-tops, or on the light verandahs usually built at the entrance to the principal apartments and open to the cool breezes. As generally in Islam among the wealthier families, the husband might have as many as four wives and a number of concubines, in addition to the female servants, all living in the harem. The men's quarters of his house would contain all the male members of the family, the black and white slaves and, if the owner were very rich, the eunuchs. The white female slaves were usually in the households of the Turkish officials; the local wealthy slave-owners preferred the girls they called 'Abyssinians', who were light brown or bronze in colour, and had fine features. They were handsome but frail, and soon succumbed to tuberculosis; they generally cost between one-third and one-tenth the price of a white slave-girl. Three days' trial was allowed on these purchases, during which time the girl stayed in the women's quarters and the ladies of the household reported on her suitability: snoring, grinding the teeth or talking in her sleep was sufficient reason to return her to the dealer. Black slaves were used for menial purposes, and the females were dearer than the males, although all who had not already had small-pox were lower in price as they were not immune to the disease which was endemic. Slaves were generally not as well treated in the provinces as in Turkey, and many were so badly handled on their journey from Africa over desert and down river through Nubia and Upper Egypt, that many children drowned themselves in the Nile during the journey.

In the town, as in the country, all rose very early and after prayers took their morning meal of flat bread, eggs, cheese or yoghurt, or perhaps beans simmered overnight in an earthenware pot buried up to the neck in hot ashes. Then the men of the family would ride out on the day's business, usually mounted on asses or mules and often accompanied by grooms who attempted to clear a way for them through the narrow streets by flailing about with a long stick and calling out warnings, although even these precautions often failed to save a rider from being swept off his mount by the overwide load of a passing camel. These beasts were in any case unpredictable, and it was a tenet of Muslim law that while any damage done by the front legs of a camel was the responsibility of the man who held its halter, no man could be answerable for what mischief might be done by its back legs. The day in shop or office was spent chatting with customers and other shopkeepers or colleagues, drinking coffee and smoking, and conducting business in an atmosphere of leisure; those men who did not work rode about visiting, or went to a hammam, and returned for a light lunch after which they retired for a rest in the private quarters from which they were never disturbed. Few people stayed up for long after the meal that followed the evening prayer: their houses were lit with small glass vessels filled with oil in which stood a wick of cotton twisted round a straw, but the light they gave was inadequate and the day's activities usually came to an end two or three hours after sunset. Life was predictably less sophisticated in small provincial towns. There were some minor arts and crafts, mainly of wood- and metal-work, but there was little demand for luxuries or encouragement of artistic effort.

The men of the better class dressed in a style not dissimilar to that of the townsmen in Turkey, with full trousers, shirt, girdled robe and caftan, with a ceremonial robe over all and a turban; in cold weather they added a black woollen cloak which could be pulled over the head. The lower class wore loose trousers, a long wide-sleeved shirt of blue linen or cotton in summer and of brown wool in winter, open from neck to waist, a red or white girdle and a coarse cotton turban over a felt cap; the poorest had simply a shirt and a cloth tied round the head. As in all Muslim countries the turban varied with the sect and occupation and was much respected. The distinguishing dress of teachers brought them all the reverence which that profession commanded, and passers-by would ask them to say a short prayer or blessing for them, and in the markets the shop-keepers would not ask the official price but accepted what they gave them. A teacher from one of the great universities, such as al-Azhar in Cairo, was often attended by the sons of rich men, two or three boys whom he would accept to act as his servants, in exchange for which he would pass on to them his wisdom and knowledge.

Women of the wealthier class wore a short loose shirt and wide trousers tied around the hips and below the knee, a long fitting caftan buttoning in front and tied with a girdle made of a folded square shawl. On the head they wore a felt cap and turban and an embroidered head veil over all, and on the feet inner and outer slippers. In the street all this was covered by a thick veil which hung from eyes to feet and a voluminous cloth, black if the woman were married and white if she were not, which covered the head and enveloped everything else. Their hair was plaited into many little thin braids, between eleven and twenty-five of them, always uneven in number, with three little black silk cords with golden ornaments attached to each braid. Their eyes were darkened heavily with kohl and their hands and feet decorated with the red stain of henna; many were tattooed on the chin and elsewhere on the face in a pattern of bluish or greenish dots. Women of the lower class wore trousers, a shirt and the face-veil and wrap, and as much cheap jewellery as they could afford: they were very fond of heavy anklets, which chinked as they walked and were considered particularly vulgar and provocative by men of religion.

The population of the eastern provinces was not exclusively Muslim: there were large communities of Jews in Palestine, some indigenous and some refugees from the religious persecutions in Spain and Portugal. They were mainly engaged in trade and in textile industries, and were frequently subject to extortion and illegal punishment by corrupt officials, who also forced them to work on Saturday, their holy day, transporting dung. The groups of Samaritans were also considered as Jews, and were similarly mistreated for 'insufficient humility': it was an unfortunate fact that remoteness from the seat of government in Istanbul and the corrupting effects of life around them not infrequently had a debasing effect on Turkish government servants.

The largest Christian community was that of the Copts of Egypt; the language of their liturgy and bible testified to their direct descent from the ancient Egyptians, and their standard of living was generally slightly higher than that of their Muslim neighbours. There were also considerable settlements of Christians in Lebanon and Palestine. In addition, there were large numbers of Christian pilgrims who came annually to visit the holy places, and these were so satisfactory a source of revenue that the shrines were well maintained and the government itself intervened when they were over-exploited by the locals. A large number of these Christian sanctuaries were visited by Muslims too, whose reverence extended to such relics of Jewish holy men as the tombs of David in Jerusalem and Moses near the Dead Sea, the tombs of the patriarchs in Hebron, and the graves of Jonah, Lot and many others; the shrine said to be the tomb of the Virgin in Jerusalem, and the church at Bethlehem, were also included in the category of Muslim holy places. But the main place of pilgrimage in Palestine remained the Rock, on which, according to tradition Abraham had been about to sacrifice his son, and, later, the Prophet Muhammad landed on his miraculous night journey; adjacent to it was the mosque al-Aqsa. The journey to these sites was only a little less meritorious than the visit to Mecca and Medina, but they were all long and difficult and the travellers had to maintain themselves on the way and liked, if possible, to show a little profit. Most of them certainly undertook the pilgrimages in a spirit of piety and religious duty, but a large number chaffered their way across the country, buying and selling at villages and towns on the way, travelling with military convoys as much because they paid no tolls as to avail themselves of protection, and trying at every step to avoid the payment of taxes; their passage was a stimulating and welcome diversion in the more peaceful districts through which they passed.

And there were countless others. For in its heyday the peoples of the empire were so numerous and varied that no complete register was ever compiled, and the great Suleyman was content to call himself:

'. . . Sultan of the Sultans of East and West, Lord born under a fortunate conjunction, of the kingdoms of the Romans and Persians and Arabs, hero of all that is, pride of the arena of earth and time; of the Mediterranean and the Black Sea, and the glorified Kaaba and the illumined Medina, the noble Jerusalem and the throne of Egypt, that rarity of the age, and the province of Yemen, and Aden and Sana, and Baghdad the abode of rectitude, and Basra and al-Hasa and the Cities of Nushiravan, and the lands of Algiers and Azerbaijan, the steppes of the Kipchak and the land of the Tatars, and Kurdistan and Luristan, and of the countries of Rumelia and Anatolia and Karaman and Wallachia and Moldavia and Hungary all together, and many more kingdoms and lands mighty of esteem: Sultan and Padishah. . . .'

GLOSSARY OF TURKISH TERMS

These definitions refer to the words as used in their context. Words which are explained where they occur in the text, and do not appear again, are not included here.

agha *senior officer, head of department*

ahi *member of socio-religious brotherhood*

bazaar *open street market*

bedesten *covered market for valuables*

Bektashi *heterodox dervish*

boza *drink made of barley and millet*

cadi *judge*

caique *long fast light boat*

caliphate *office of Successor of the Prophet*

caravanserai *see* khan

charshi *covered market*

dervish *member of religious mystical order*

devshirme *levy of boys from the subject peoples*

Divan *Council, Law Court*

ezan *the call to prayer*

Fatiha *opening chapter of the Koran*

Grand Vizier *Sultan's Chief Minister*

gulbenk *chanted invocation to God, prayer for the Sultan*

hafiz *one who has memorised the Koran*

hajji *pilgrim*

hammal *porter, carrier*

hammam *bath-house*

harem *women of the household*

haremlik *women's quarters*

helva *sweetmeat made of sesame or semolina, and honey*

hoja *teacher*

imam *head of local Muslim community, prayer-leader*

Islam *religion of the Muslims*

jami *large mosque*

janissary *slave soldiers, originally devshirme boys*

jinn *supernatural being*

Kaaba *the shrine at Mecca*

kalfa *senior maid-servant*

kanun *law made by the Sultan*

Karagöz *puppet shadow theatre, named for its chief character*

khan *warehouse, hospice for travellers*

Khan *Lord*

kilim *woven rug*

Koran *the sacred book of Islam*

Kurban Bayram *Day of Sacrifice*

mahalle *quarter, district*

medrese *religious college attached to mosque*

mehter *official band of musicians*
mesjid *small local mosque*
Mevlevi *whirling dervish*
mihrab *empty niche in mosque,
  marking the direction of Mecca*
millet *religious community*
minaret *tower of mosque from
  which the call to prayer is recited*
minber *pulpit*
muezzin *mosque official who gives
  call to prayer*
mufti *jurisconsult*
Muslim *follower of the Prophet
  Muhammad*
nargileh *hubble-bubble pipe,
  hookah*
Osmanli *Ottoman, dynasty
  descended from Osman, and its
  subjects*
Padishah *Emperor*
pasha *Lord*
pekmez *grape molasses*
pilaff *rice dish*
Ramadan *sacred month of fasting*
selamlik *men's quarters*
Seljuk *Turkish dynasty which
  preceded the Ottomans in
  Anatolia*

serai *palace*
sharia *sacred law of Islam*
sheikh *elder, head of religious
  order or guild*
Sheikh-ul-Islam *Chief Mufti of
  the Empire*
Sherīf of Mecca *senior
  representative of the house of the
  Prophet*
shia *the sect of Muslims who hold
  that the succession to the Prophet
  passed through the line of his
  son-in-law Ali*
sipahis *feudal cavalry*
sunni *majority division of Muslims
  who revere Ali as the third caliph
  but do not admit that the caliphate
  runs exclusively in his line*
tandur *table over a stove and
  covered with a quilt*
tughra *Sultan's monogram*
ulema *religious functionaries,
  established heads of law and
  religion*
waqf *charitable endowment*
yuruk *nomad*
Zemzem *holy well and spring in
  Mecca*

Index

INDEX

INDEX

205